From the Editor 2020

Pacific Daily Times Editorials

Jesse Steele

Amazon Paperback Edition

books.jessesteele.com

books@jessesteele.com

ISBN 979-8589181500

For MBI

Table of Contents

2020 Preface

Many thought of this past year as a hardship. Indeed, it was. But, 2020 was not without its shining moments of beauty and heroism, nor did it lack valuable learning.

As from the beginning, I spent the year in Taiwan. Especially this year, many in the West no longer confuse Taiwan with Thailand. Taiwan is a Mandarin-speaking island harboring the runaway government from the unfinished Chinese Communist revolution. Thailand is a Thai-speaking nation on the Asian mainland bordering Vietnam. I didn't know the difference either when I arrived.

Earlier this year, protests broke out in Hong Kong. Nearly all places of protest that appeared in global news outlets are places I have been to in person. Knowing the culture of the Hong Kong people, this was something I understood on a personal level; I did not need anyone to educate me on the complexities of the situation. Instead, I spent my weeks educating the West.

As many prefaces in this series state, my uncle warned me about the Chinese. 2020's unveiling of China's bullish values was not a surprise to everyone. I aimed to educate readers so it would be less surprising in the future.

But, PDT is not in league with mainstream news. There has always been a clear agenda in selecting which news stories to publish. Indeed, PDT has a narrative so readers can follow and understand our times as they unfold, but this is different from an agenda steered through selective censorship. By looking at the evident agenda of the mainstream news league—both the lockstep repetitive reporting of the same, few events and the loud and the consistent silence on things which should concern readers—PDT editorials map out where the global news agenda is trying to direct the public. Clearly, Western news audiences were being conditioned to support war with China. Was this good or bad? I have no opinion other than that war with China was foreseeable.

Times' editorials aimed to decrease the number of people who are surprised by history unfolding. This is not limited to China, but also to the events in America. In 2015 when Trump announced his candidacy, I decided he would win both 2016 and 2020. In the February 3 editorial, I said that his margin would increase. According to mathematical and procedural analysis, it did. Even with this year's election in dispute, in the December 21 editorial, I predicted that Congress's certification of the electoral college come early January 2021 will likely lead to Trump having a second term.

I don't have a crystal ball to see future events through. Instead I look toward the future through the eyes of history. My hope is that in reading editorials from the Times, you can do the same on your own.

Editor Notes

These articles were originally published to online readers on the dates indicated. They were collected and first made available in this printed format in early 2021. In this printed edition, they have neither been reviewed nor edited. While these articles aim to be useful and informative, as editorials, they are not news, but *comment* on the news, and never at any time have they, nor any part of this book, made any claim as to fact.

The names of various editorial series follow musical terms, hence they are collectively called *Symphony*.

The *Voice* series is a "think piece" analysis of current events and is often irregular.

The theme of *Prelude* is that a military conflict was on its way. When shots were fired over the Myanmar-China border, I decided that the prelude in Asia was ended and that the conflict had begun.

The theme of *Cadence* is that a military conflict marches on, evident and already present, though it may still seem orderly.

The theme of *Encore* is that good days of renaissance, revival, renewal, reconciliation, and revitalization of a nation and its people are clearly on their way. It is not only the song itself, but also the applause leading to it.

Articles by Date

2020

Encore of Revival: America, January 6

Happy New Year! Free speech is threatened most when it is laid down freely. It is threatened more when public companies are allowed to threaten it. Prior to Hong Kong protests, the term "self-censorship" was tossed around like a fourth-grade sponge ball on a PhysEd parachute. Today, if Facebook doesn't want someone's name mentioned —even though the people not allowed to mention the name aren't involved—then Facebook users won't mention the name for fear of losing their connection to friends and family.

That is the usual blackmail, right?—friends and family?

Pacific Daily Times will not report the name of an ousted whistleblower unless it either becomes old news and is needed for discussion or there is litigation involving the whistleblower. But, that's as far as things go. Should enough time pass or the whistleblower file private or civil action over being mentioned—or a disenfranchised social media user were to file private or civil action over being censored or banned—then the name becomes fair game for the Times. For the Times, it's about being niche and newsworthy rather than alarmist and chasing the most recent fad. We want a name attached to a story that is unusual from what others will report.

But, Facebook, YouTube, and others in mainline media seem to have more in the game than just keeping things relevant and interesting. Banning users and removing content for naming a name already named seems to indicate that they are protecting the whistleblower because they support what the whistleblower did. That stacks up the best, anyway.

At the Times, others being banned for repeating the named name is far more interesting than the name itself. Banning or censoring users for mentioning an ousted whistleblower on publicly listed social media platforms is atrocious. We are headed for public utilitization of social media. The same could be argued for food, drug, and grocery giants, but that's another editorial for another week.

This raises another question. What is a "whistleblower" anyway? Generally, the term is vernacular, referring to someone who sees foul play and "blows a whistle". The problem is that whistleblowers wear special clothes to identify themselves, wave flags with bright colors, and make loud noises to draw the attention of an entire stadium. But, ever since Trump threatened an inbred political swamp in one of the most white-collar corrupt graft cities in the world, the term "whistleblower" seems to have been reassigned the definition "accuser in hiding who has a right to accuse without proof, then keep hiding".

This "whistleblower" isn't the actual whistleblower but a spectator in the stands. By the standard definition, the real whistleblowers were the Federal agents who acted upon the claims. Misapplying the term "whistleblower" to this anonymous, baseless coward of an accuser has only served to lionize the housecat.

Cadence of Conflict: Asia, January 6

The West has been at odds with the Far East for centuries. It began before the Opium Wars, laws and treaties were made and broken, but the issues remain the same old same old. Chinese stare down their noses at the rest of the world, regardless of the imbalance it causes for their end of the teeter-totter we all stand on. They believe China getting richer and expanding its borders is fair for them, and whatever may or may not be unfair for the rest of the world doesn't matter because justice is only a matter of importance in whether Chinese receive justice. Everyone else can either become Chinese or die—which would do their miserable existence a favor. That is the ancient worldview driving the Far East to do what it has always done—what it continues to do today.

But, one thing is different now: Not all Chinese speakers go along with Chinese supremacism. Previously, dissidents who had been crushed by Chinese supremacism were either Uncle Toms in their own rite or too scared to object, but not anymore. Hong Kong is standing up to old generation arrogance, so is Taiwan. People within Hong Kong and Taiwan are standing up to that arrogance even within their cultures, families, social circles, and societies at large. That old supremacism is collapsing at the hands of free-thinking, self-motivated, self-initiated Chinese-speakers themselves, Cantonese speakers of the same historic culture notwithstanding the least. The "Revolution of Our Times" is much deeper that Hong Kong political identity; it's cultural, regional, and even global. Consider Chinatowns and Chinese churches across America—which won't be any kind of exception.

Soon, Trump will have something to hang over everyone's head—Democrats and Chinese Communists alike. It's a power stronger than any missile. Next week, China is sending a delegation to sign the infamously famous "Phase 1". Woohoo!

Encore of Revival: America, January 13

The Iranian government's alibi—or "explanation", rather—of how it shot down a passenger jet from Ukraine is entirely believable. Barring some grandiose conspiracy, there would be no imaginable motive for any government—friend or foe, even a terrorist sponsor like Iran—to use government assets to kill civilians.

The Iranian military's story is believable to any Westerner who has spend more than three years in a first-world or second-world country. Sadly, poorer parts of America have similar cultures, poorer White communities as well as minorities. Any autocratic, bossy, domineering culture can easily make severe miscalculations. They do it in Sunday morning congregations all the time.

According to CNN, according to Iran, their government was on high alert, then misidentified a plane from Ukraine as it turned toward a Revolutionary Guard base. In sum, that led to a snap judgment, what Iran calls "human error". The Iranian government wants to put systems in place to avoid such miscalculations in the future. In the West, we call that "growing up"—learning how to not make rush judgements.

While Iran's story is believable to any Western expat with experience in a developing country, most Americans don't know the degree to which immature people run many governments of the world. Part of being a first-world nation means that people in the government need to be mature.

Iran learning from its mistake could be the most significant turning point where Iran's government learns the "confident humility" needed to govern with maturity. If that happens, Sec. Mike Pompeo's goal of Iran behaving "like a normal country" will come true. Iran claimed that their military was on high alert in the first place because of tensions surrounding the strike in Iraq. In short, killing Qassem Soleimani helped Iran.

Now, the task is for Americans to understand other people enough to understand why being immature cost the lives of 176 people. Whether at home, the office, or in government, immaturity is the source of much injustice—a lesson which Americans will learn, eventually.

Cadence of Conflict: Asia, January 13

The overwhelming, earth-shattering, landslide re-election victory of Taiwan's President Tsai Ing-Wen sends a shocking message to Beijing: If you plan to take Taiwan, prepare for greater opposition than you got from Hong Kong. But, like the house cat who doesn't know it's not God, let alone that it's not any tiger, they won't ever decrypt the message. Beijing will be emotionally hurt, insulted, and will thus froth with rage.

Choosing former Premier William Lai as her Vice running mate was wise. Not only is he loved for—perhaps only for—his intractable stance against corruption, he also views Taiwan as having an already de facto independent status. While President Tsai prefers status quo—a peacefully unresolved dispute with China—Vice President Elect Lai views any Taiwanese declaration of independence from China as no more than a formality for how things already are anyway.

This choice of William Lai strengthens her position. If she were to step down, a president would take her place with an even stronger stance against Chinese expansionism. So, even her political opponents would want her to remain in office.

Taiwan's position is stronger, not only in US relations, but also within Taiwan. Expect actions from China that result in Taiwan responding with moves toward even greater independence than status quo already boasts.

Encore of Revival: America, January 20

Current events are forcing everyone into a deep state of soul-searching. Some Iranians were angry after Trump's drone strike, mourning the death of a leader they somehow admired. They didn't blame Americans, except that they did. Once the Iranian government admitted to shooting down the passenger jet from Ukraine, Iranians en masse took to the streets, protesting the current government.

As Symphony explained last week, some leaders have yet to "grow up" more than others. Those with more growing up to go tend to invite resentment from those they lead. Iran was no exception. Authoritarianism led to the mistake with the passenger jet, but it also allowed certain leaders to rise in the first place, one whom was killed by a drone strike approved by President Trump.

In America, the doomed impeachment articles from the House were so evidently unpopular that their true purpose went on parade: a parade. Yes, it was only ever for show. So, when House Democrats were forced to give the Republican Senate what they did not want, they continued the show for their supporters' own entertainment.

But, the show isn't done yet. Irritation and aggravation will only rise higher and higher as the nation sees what's really going on. That could be said for both Iranians and Americans.

Cadence of Conflict: Asia, January 20

China is engaging in "rapid expansionism"; this is different from the slower-moving modes of Russia and, until Trump, the United States. During Obama, Russia took back Crimea—after that fling Nikita Khrushchev had in giving Crimea to Ukraine when it wasn't his to give. Russia has also been crawling its influence in Syria, softly with Iran, and shrewdly using China as an effective puppet.

America, though not an empire seeking to claim more within its political borders, propelled power through military bases around the world. Once the Chinese got over their phobia of technology—a disease it long had, which even led up to the Opium Wars—they looked beyond their bubble and saw America's non-border expansion. But, they still haven't seen Russia's soft-handed expansion for what it is. 180 military bases in China's backyard didn't bode well with China's neediness for receiving endless heinie kisses.

Thankfully, Trump is slowly recalling propelled American power—consider Syria, Afghanistan, Turkey, and now Iraq. He is not the archetypal "neocon" expansionist. But, other than Trump, America did have its own soft form of expansionism.

China, different from either of the two soft expansions of America and Russia, is engaging in a more rapid, rude, speedy expansion. The Chinese don't care how they come across to others because they have been knocked off their emotional rockers, having seen that the world doesn't regard them to be a fraction of what they think themselves to be. This speed has alarmed the nations of the world like a body's immune system responding to a spreading virus or cancer. Even India is on alert.

Russia played its card well—or maybe we should say Russia played its China well: expansion backed by Russia, which upsets the global balance, and Russia doesn't get blamed for it. China doesn't know what its speedy expansion, mainly against Taiwan and India, will do because China hasn't been paying attention to the rest of the world for most of human history.

Encore of Revival: America, January 27

The concept of an ongoing impeachment process against every sitting president isn't that bad of an idea. In some governments, it's the fourth branch of government called the "Control". Perhaps Obama, Bush, and Clinton—all the way to FDR and Wilson—would have served the people better if they had an ongoing impeachment proceeding. It's tempting, but, for now anyway, it looks like a big waste of time.

The president's defense seems incredibly boring, but that won't matter. The Democratic prosecution omits key evidence, but that won't matter either. Every vote in the Senate has already been decided. These proceedings contain the platform for the other side to be added where there was only one side of what should be fair. Life isn't fair, but drama stops at the Senate floor. As with Clinton, there is neither basis to remove Trump from Office. Impeachment is a big deal, but usually falls to the popular opinion; voting citizens are the jury. Both times, all the energy from the House was spent on the Senate, which just let the House wear itself tired.

While one proceeding moves forward for show toward a pre-agreed verdict, another investigation continues against the faction that wanted this impeachment in the first place. A network of unhappy people from the opposite side of the political spectrum, largely in cahoots with the FBI and beyond, tried to prevent a president from being elected, then tried to remove him from office for something that didn't happen. In their view, justice is an illusion; they only do what suits them with whatever power they have. For them, might is morally right. Fortunately, democracies have systems in place to prevent power-defined morality touted by Leftist activists in America's legal justice system—whether judges or FBI.

The strongest evidence in this impeachment trial is the phone call read-out between Trump and Zelensky. It only seems inditing when heard in small snippets by people who hate Trump anyway. To everyone else, it is acquitting. Calling witnesses would stretch on and on and, for Republicans, would only serve the purpose of exposing the swamp that the FBI was a small part of. Democrats gamble that the Senate won't call witnesses, so House managers taunt the Senate about not calling witnesses. But, just how the president released the contents of the phone conversation by surprise, the Senate could decide to start the boring process of asking pre-written questions through the Chief Justice. The main purpose for Republicans would be to put accomplices on the stand. If that happens, expect at the top of the list the center of the phone call's discussion: Joe Biden.

Cadence of Conflict: Asia, January 27

Trying to be polite or indirect while not taking no for an answer does not give anyone a right to make trouble. When someone gives a decisive, "No," decent people accept that answer, then move on somehow. But, China doesn't seem able to do that. In Beijing's thought, relentlessly pushing forward, no matter how many more thousands hate them by the day, China is being polite to Hong Kong. They are being indirect. By not giving up, the Chinese Communists believe they have very politely told Hong Kongers how things will be, thereby justifying whatever manslaughter China chooses to invoke.

It's not as if China has a lot of time to worry about telling other people what to do. Hong Kong was designed in its Basic Law to be largely autonomous. That means that Hong Kong can take care of itself, should China need to put energies into other matters—such as stopping the African swing flu or the Wuhan coronavirus.

China's choices led to a landslide re-election for the de facto independence president of Taiwan. She says there is no independence to declare because Taiwan can't possibly be any more independent than it already is. Some in Beijing might think that means Taiwan has reached its limit; but anyone in the West knows that means Taiwan already has the fullest measure of independence as defined. Yes, many in Beijing might not know that.

Vietnam reached a similar vague point in gearing up for military strength in ASEAN. Buying boats from India is also on Vietnam's agenda—yes, India is another country China has managed to aggravate.

Why do things unfold this way in China's back yard? It's not that China is so much evil as it is immature. But, we tend to stay immature when we age, if we won't open up to the outside world. Rather than helping China learn, the West just dumped money and emboldened a brat, all so we could save a few pennies on our stuff. Who is really being the most unfair to who? Friends know when to accept a no because friends know when to say, "No."

Encore of Revival: America, February 3

After hearing from the house managers and then the Trump defense team, it sounds more like the one who may have committed "high crimes and misdemeanors" would be Joe Biden. Maxim Waters claimed that impeachment is not governed by law, only whatever whim Congress decides—a statement that simply isn't true.

This level of lawlessness expected of the government suggests a nation doomed. A growing portion of the electorate actually believe that government should take whatever drastic action it wants—because they feel comfortable with the current action proposed. But, they so quickly forget that the tables were only recently reversed, and being lawful in the very way they hold in contempt now was the only thing protecting them from the government doing likewise to them just a few years ago.

The biggest danger Trump always posed was that he would do too good of a job, that he would be too successful, and that the Republicans would thus earn great power that they neither deserved nor understood. These past few months, Republicans have announced that they would back a president they abhorred just a few years ago. They do this because they enjoy the success they didn't expect him to create because they had failed to create that success at anytime in their careers. Hateful yesterday, grateful today, what will tomorrow hold for Republicans?

Last week, as expected, Republicans turned down Democrats' call for more witnesses—after House Democrats could have called the same witnesses, but didn't. Though having Biden on record would have played well in Republican politics, the disgruntled, disenfranchised, dejected, and shamed former National Security Advisor John Bolton was never going to be given a soapbox. He is a war monger and a neo-Conservative, still angry that Trump pulled out of Syria and Afghanistan. Democrats wanted him as a witness, but Republicans knew he would only yield opinion and tainted facts at best, understandably contrary to the president who fired him. That was never going to happen and Democrats knew it; that's why Democrats asked for it. Getting rejected often rallies the voter base.

As Democrats push their case for impeachment because of "feelings rather than law", Republican voters are rallying around their president. Trump will likely win by an even greater margin in 2020 than he did in 2016, all thanks to the support for impeachment. This is not only because of Democrats on Capitol Hill. In coffee shops, offices, and homes, Republican voters are listening to Democrat voters give their reasons to support impeachment and that scares them just as much, if not more, than what Democrats in Washington say. Thus, in 2020, the Senate stands to gain even more seats, inching ever closer to a supermajority in the Senate. Once that happens, our liberties will be at the greatest risk since the founding because nothing is as dangerous as a party not held in check. Republicans in Washington pose a supermajority danger to all voters, and it was Democratic voters who helped it all happen—because their parents never taught them why government must not be lawless.

Cadence of Conflict: Asia, February 3

The world is fed up with China's Communist Party, including people in China. The Wuhan virus is a blame-blaming scandal of a magnitude greater than Chairman Mao. It could crack the foundation of Xi Jinping's rule and party confidence along with it.

Top down leadership ties the hands of first responders. So does propaganda-driven speech censorship. Of course an outbreak will breakout where people aren't allowed to respond or warn without permission from the central bureaucracy. For China, it was only a matter of time.

And, the world is fed up. Now Hong Kong, severely underprepared for an outbreak, faces a strike of 6k medical workers and growing—if CEO Carrie Lam doesn't completely close the Hong Kong border to China. Simply not having the resources to handle an outbreak should be enough for Hong Kong to to close its border. Not doing what simply should be done begs more questions of whether Beijing's top down leadership is preventing Hong Kong from responding to the Wuhan outbreak, which would be yet another violation of the Basic Law and a breach of China's treaty with Britain that allowed Hong Kong to return.

Shameless in the face of its mismanagement in Wuhan then Hong Kong, China then asked the EU for emergency medical supplies. The EU would be wise to respond that giving medical supplies would require proper oversight, including an end to the bureaucratic methods of centralized control that delayed containment in Wuhan and keeps Hong Kong in danger. Also, the EU should require China to stop politicizing Taiwan's need to join the World Health Organization.

Argument could be made that Taiwan and the West are capitalizing on the Wuhan crisis to get more international recognition for Taiwan. But, then it could also be argued that China created that need to capitalize on a crisis to do something that should have been done long ago. In light of the Wuhan outbreak, Canada, Japan, and the EU now sponsor Taiwan's request to join the World Health Organization as an active participant, not a mere observer. A viral White House petition snowballed past the threshold over the weekend, effectively making the same request of President Trump. Now that Trump has a massive petition to respond to, China won't be able to claim "interference" when he responds. But, China may try to anyway because, in Confucian Communist thinking, petitions of the people should be ignored.

Encore of Revival: America, February 10

Trump's acquittal did not come because of party politics or friends in Washington. It came because he stood fast—he held his ground in a party that tried to denounce him early on. He had many good friends helping, but it was Trump himself that empowered their efforts and directed the flow.

The Republican Party is not what it seems. They hated Trump when he didn't do things in their failing manner, but now they acquit him and act like they have always been BFF from the beginning. Any disagreements in Trump's early days don't matter anymore, even though that's not the tone they used at the time, though a number of those Republicans are out of office.

It's typical. The Republicans held their noses while Reagan gave them success. They passed Democratic-oriented, anti-Conservative laws during the W. Bush years viz the Patriot Act. They objected to Conservative voices in media during the 2005 "Build a Fence" movement viz Senator Lott. Thanks to Trump's inability to be railroaded, they are being gifted more success and clout than they ever didn't earn before.

Senator McConnell stayed true to the colors he flew, which is more than can be said for the late Senator McCain or Senator Romney, who took his

unofficial place as "Republican Senate maverick".
Senator Romney's departure from the fold could
make him a one-term Senator—and not from lack
of RNC backing. Senator Graham and many others
took their stand for law, order, facts, evidence,
process, and truth. The Republican Party stood
behind their president, this time. Had former
House Republicans not been card-carrying
members of the metaphorical "never Trumper"
movement, Republicans might still hold the House
and none of this ugly impeachment would have
happened.

Justice came from Republicans this time; don't get
used to it. While Democrats are the party of hate
and failed "we wanna' help you" platitudes, the
Republicans are the party of treachery. Democrats
stand together while Republicans usually don't. It
was a strange week in Washington. Things will be
fine through the Trump years because they will
depend on him. But after that, buckle up.

Cadence of Conflict: Asia, February 10

The words of US President Trump set an unsettling policy for Communist China: "We're also getting our allies, finally, to help pay their fair share." This is far-reaching.

By having multiple nations with multiple militaries operating with appropriate budgets, China faces an enclave of opponents, not just one. There is no single head to decapitate. If you're in Beijing, sitting in a room filled with Mandarin speakers who agree that they are entitled to make the world their servant, Trump's words scare you.

While Beijing fights the virus it tried to cover up, Taiwan had recorded 10 deaths from that virus. Yet, China reported 13 in Taiwan, then told the United Nations that China speaks accurately for Taiwan, still arguing that Taiwan should not enter the WHO—even taking offense, still, at any suggestion of entry. Taiwanese Foreign Minister Wu pointed out that the WHO has referred to Taiwan by at least three different names in reporting on China's Wuhan outbreak. This week, even the US spoke up for Taiwan's request to join the WHO; China was all the more offended.

The outbreak isn't fairing well for China's credibility in governing Hong Kong either. Supermarkets are full of empty shelves.

While China's central government will continue the playbook strategy of blaming the very local governments it dominates, the central government's solution to the failure of a centralized government will be to centralize more government. In Confucian Communism, control is the solution to every problem, especially the problems that control causes. So they themselves believe even more than they purport, the reason that China has so many challenges within its vast stretches of land is that it doesn't have even more land. The Chinese Communists believe that their number one problem is that they don't control the world.

Encore of Revival: America, February 17

Democrats and Republicans are working in evil tandem. In a sense, Republicans have no choice. The attacks against Conservatives in America are so extreme and unfair that our laws might not be suited to defend us from them. Going easy on Roger Stone in his punishment for something that wasn't wrong seems like playing favorites, from more than one angle. It's okay when Democrats do it, but when Democratic Washington attacks men for less than John Brennan has done wrong it seems like those men must be unfair in order to receive justice.

We are in a spiral of decay.

Pure democracy is sheer tyranny of the masses, allowing the 51% to gang up on the 49%. But, a Democratic Republic, like the USA, doesn't—or shouldn't—allow the 99% to gang up on the 1% because every single person has rights that no one else can take away. But, in attempts to punish famous people for supporting a candidate in the "other political party", and in LGBTQ trying to change the rules of restrooms and use prison to punish people for grammar rules without classic literature, we are seeing the 1% try to gang up on the 99%. Some, not all, of the Left want an aristocracy that they steer.

But, it doesn't stop there. While a few in the Left try to gang up on the ever-less-so-silent majority, huge backlash is coming even against more moderate Liberals. The public-funding-driven Liberals, different from the social-driven Liberals, are getting a bad wrap from the Right. People are being hated for believing things they don't believe on both sides of the political spectrum. While the Right is rising up against the Far Left, another backlash is coming back against the Right in the more distant future. That will be when the nation's institutions are shaken, in the days when we all are forced to listen to each other—in the days when the nation's inner turmoil sees daylight and we find our hearts.

Cadence of Conflict: Asia, February 17

The 2019-nCoV Wuhan virus isn't doing any good for Xi Jinping's public trust. Dissidents inside China are silenced and their social media accounts scrubbed. Joshua Wong issues a call to arms from Hong Kong. Taiwan closes its border and plans to evacuate its citizens from the quarantined cruise ship, Diamond Princess. Yet, the Philippines blocks entry to Taiwanese airline passengers while in-flight because World Health Organization information reports Taiwan as part of China. And, Xi tells Trump that everything will be okay after April's hot weather kills the virus.

It looks like the world wants a fight. Why did evacuation plans for this cruise ship take so long? Why doesn't China close its border to Hong Kong as an act of good faith to at least pretend to want to earn public trust? China locked down Wuhan and Huanggang, why not Shenzhen?

The WHO praised China's efforts, claiming they bought the world time. That doesn't stack— information control started the problem, China's clampdown on information only grows, the Philippines close their border to a country run by a completely different administration on account of the WHO reporting in denial. Is the WHO controlled by China, does the WHO just want to start a war, or could it be that the WHO wants to start a war because it doesn't like being controlled by China?

Fear of the virus may be overrated. Initial figures suggested that the seasonal flu may be more deadly. But, panic is panic. And, with Chinese cities going on lockdown, countries closing borders, and hundreds of people getting sick on a cruise ship after it was quarantined, nerves are on edge. Chinese State control of information has been exposed for the hoax it is; no Chinese people will trust China's government again. Even those who support the Communist Party can't expect the public to believe them anymore, no matter what they say. In the middle of the breakdown of Chinese trust and control, Xi's solution is to fly bombers around Taiwan.

Nothing re-elects a president like a war someone else started and nothing fires a president like an outbreak or a failed economy. If Xi invades Taiwan, Trump's re-election will be even more certain and Xi's own party could be doomed along with him. Nothing would weaken China's People's Liberation Army at home like the decision to boost its political image by invading one of the best responding WHO-non-members in the world, Taiwan. Xi is so addicted to failing, self-destructive decisions, invading Taiwan might be the ultimate fatal flaw of failure that he just can't refuse. While this viral outbreak isn't quite enough to push Xi to the point of desperation for distraction, it's another bail of hay on the camel's back.

Encore of Revival: America, February 24

At what point is a government agency no longer allowed to invent a fake crime that was not committed, investigate people known to be innocent for this known-to-be-fake crime, then imprison those people investigated for taking steps to survive that agency breaking the law?

Afghani peace progressing in the wake of home-bound American troops is carrying Trump to an even greater landslide second term. But, it's not enough to distract from the FBI's damage to its own reputation. With Bernie Sanders as the Democratic nominee apparent, and knowing that his base hates government corruption as much as they want to bring troops home, talk of government agency abuse will be so high in the upcoming election that avoiding fundamental changes to the FBI will be unavoidable. To say the least, Comey overreached.

The American Left, along with the closet Left in the political establishment, is loosing their grip on themselves, now that they've lost their grip on government. They want to accuse a man of something that didn't happen, then call a witness, and, if that witness denies the events of what didn't happen, accuse that witness of lying. Such a witness was about to be thrown in prison, Roger

Stone, at the age of 67. People who believe that
what didn't happen didn't happen intervened and
stopped him from being thrown in prison for
alleged lies in an investigation that shouldn't have
happened.

Today on the Left, voters and elected officials alike,
are angry about Roger Stone not going to prison.
His true crime is not lying to the FBI, but being a
friend of the president they don't like. The line that
distinguishes voters who want him in prison from
those who don't isn't a line that runs along
boundaries of an FBI investigation, but a line
between voters who believe there was Russian
corruption with Trump in 2016 and those who do
not.

They had their impeachment and trial. They didn't
get the outcome they wanted. Now, they are
pushing evermore, all the while telling themselves
that they are saving the country. Little do they
know or realize that it is party politics, and the
idea that only an irrelevant few hold a different
view, that endangers America. This was supposed
to be a country of respect between people who
disagree. But, now we see the truth: Christians
and non-Christians were never going to be able to
get along because the non-Christians wouldn't
allow it. And, I'm not defining a Christian as a
"Sunday morning attendee". The Bible-based value
of "love for enemies" and giving fair treatment to
the opposition is unique to Christians.
Interestingly, so it is between the Right and Left of
America. Perhaps this is a foreshadowing of the

coming global conflict and the even greater conflict
between God's Holy Angels and the Satanic, fallen
rebellion that has lasted thousands of years.

Cadence of Conflict: Asia, February 24

There isn't news this week. More countries hate China. More people are sick with Wuhan nCoV. Cases rise in the Far East. Taiwan is one of the safest places to be—in terms of the virus, that is. Friends of Taiwan continue to be punished; this week regarded Czech in particular with the Senate chair planning a visit to one of the safest places to be in the Far East—in terms of the virus, that is.

The trend in Western journalism is to look down the nose toward China. Media censorship, mismanagement, discontent, and incompetence are part of the narrative. The US president has a different take.

Satellite-based data has been used to suggest that China may be burning thousands of bodies in Wuhan. The site that aggregated the data that was separately used to make this suggestion was windy.com—a Czech company. Go figure. Windy.com did not make the suggestion; it visually animates data already available to the public. There is no news here, only everyone's data and someone else's speculation. The interesting part is how quick the Western public is to jump on any excuse to think something bad about China.

Certainly, cynicism toward China is not without cited history. China remains indignant. Nothing is new, except Czech's name in the headlines. China's spite for Taiwan and friends only grows as spite for China and friends snowballs all the more. Perhaps next week will yield something new in the news. But, when so many people are so bound to make history repeat, there just might not be much to report—except for those who only read what repeats.

Encore of Revival: America, March 2

Tom Steyer doesn't seem to know which party he's running for. Recommending private sector solutions to the voter base that wanted Sanders v Trump in 2016 is, in a word, nutty. But, he shares one thing in common with Bloomberg: they think Trump's deep pockets bought him the election, so they could copy-cat the same victory. But, Trump's deep pockets didn't buy him the election; Trump earned it through a life in the office rather than a private palace and over a decade of experience watching the public respond to him on camera.

While the Democratic party is being commandeered by radicals, the base is shifting from "help us -ists" to "socialists". Sanders would have probably won the 2016 nomination were it not for the Democratic party's non-democratic system of superdelegates throwing their minority support to Hillary. Unlike the professional campaign organizers (including Biden), and unlike the lazy rich guys (including Biden), Sanders is the real deal. He's in it because he believes in it. And, his base respects him for the same two reasons Trump's base respects him: hard work and personal connection to the crowd. To boot, it's about ideology.

Part of the schism forming between the evermore so apparent "two Americas" is about how we view money. Some view money as having an ethereal source—once a country or company is "rich", money just grows on trees or something. Others view money as having to be generated from a combination of work and savvy, no matter how rich a country or company gets. The "ethereals" believe the economy grows because government injects money from the imaginary hole in space through which money pours without end, and this is good because rich companies are purportedly rich because they have access to a similar money hole in space. The "savvyists" believe government can only give what government already took away and that companies can only make what they continue to think and work for.

The test of the 2020 election is a battle of ideals. Whichever voter base sees the universe correctly will have the strength to muster an election victory. So, you see, 2020 is about clear vision.

Cadence of Conflict: Asia, March 2

Wuhan 2019-nCoV will not end the world. But, it is throwing the world into panic. The long-time NIAID director steps out of lock with the president and gives a sobering warning about how viruses actually spread. Bad as the truth is, the stock market is drastically overreacting and Trump is trying to prevent a panic—or that's at least what we're all supposed to think. We can't have the truth of both bad and good news told to a public that dwells on the bad and ignores the good. Presidents know that, disease directors not so much. So, the director should get the muzzle, right?

That will cause more panic. Where panic and fear of China weren't enough to keep Americans from making China rich at Walmart for decades, fear of China's virus spreading at Walmart is making up for lost panic.

This is the perfect storm for those who chose not to prepare. The virus won't kill the world, but the world is panicking and will carry a grudge for what a Chinese virus did to the stock market. Once the virus passes, the world will have time to clean house. China will be blamed, as it should for it's mismatched priorities, then the world will cut

China down to the size it never should have been allowed to grow past.

But in the meantime, the Chinese people are re-evaluating their own priorities, deciding whether their president has his own priorities in order. We could be looking at more killing fields, where citizens who fell for the games of self-censorship and spreading Communist propaganda are executed as cowards. Hopefully it won't come to that. But, China will face the enemies that it made on the inside while it also faces the enemies that made it big from the outside.

Encore of Revival: America, March 9

Though he still would have lost, Sanders would have been the best candidate against Trump because he represents everything Trump is not. But, either the DNC establishment or the country doesn't side with Sanders's socialist values. In all likelihood, the DNC move away from Bernie is related to its move away from other hardline socialists in their ranks. In other words, the battle of ideologies might already be over.

The 2020 election is now in full swing. Even the Wuhan 2019-nCoV coronavirus demands a response to please November. Perhaps that's why Democrats defended Joe Biden so avidly during the impeachment process. Perhaps they always planned to have him as their front runner and nominee. Perhaps they know that socialism loses elections, even more since capitalism has been given an extra try over the last three years.

Cadence of Conflict: Asia, March 9

Things are fairing worse and worse for China, but better and better for Taiwan.

The KMT-Nationalist party is abandoning its long-standing agreement to cooperate with the Chinese Communists, much how the American Democratic party is abandoning socialism within its ranks. Taiwan's handling of the 2019-nCoV Wuhan virus is top notch, possibly the best in the world. The irony is that Taiwan is not a member of the WHO, for mere reasons of political pressure from China. The world will interpret Taiwan's absence from the WHO through the poor response to the virus from WHO members. And the world will, accordingly, blame China not only for the virus, but for the lack of Taiwan's valued input in the WHO.

This week, when things seemed as though they couldn't get worse in China, a hotel collapsed, which housed many people being observed for the virus. Not all had been diagnosed, but at least 10 are dead from the collapse.

Interestingly, this does not fair well for Taiwan. The more respect Taiwan earns from the international community, and the more spite China earns from the international community, the more envy will boil and bubble as China froths with rage against Taiwan. China's government is not functioning with any trace of sobriety. Recent events are pushing the Chinese government over the edge in their ancient desire to invade Taiwan. While that would leave them vulnerable at home and hated even more throughout the world, such things never stopped them before and certainly aren't stopping them now.

Encore of Revival: America, March 16

There is more likely to be death in America from the shortages caused by hoarding than from what should be called the "pneumoniavirus". Americans have too often harbored a love for drama. They don't want to listen when told to wash their hands or wear a mask to the supermarket when they feel sick, but when they actually realize that they can't ignore a thing, it's time to turn every home into a survival bunker. There's little sense for calm and order.

That was the deeper weakness in the societal immune system of America. Love for bad news will be the undoing of many Americans. Once this is over, the toilet paper hoarders will become known to their friends, scorned by their friends, then feel foolish. Theatrics and drama are far from over.

The economy is taking a hit—everyone is taking a hit. People will have to forgive those who overreacted, otherwise they will be the ones who overreact next.

The economic problem in America has roots deeper than the virus, but in society. And, society's problem is rooted in the spiritual. Like Lincoln during the Civil War, Trump called a day for nation-wide prayer. Anyone who so chooses will come through this better off.

Cadence of Conflict: Asia, March 16

News around the world has blacked out. Everything is about this new virus that should be called the "pneumoniavirus", also known as Wuhan's 2019-nCoV, everything—the news, the politics, the economy, the maps, organ harvesting. But, that wasn't the only Western bad news on China. Canada had a brilliant solution to the Huawei controversy: go public. So far that hasn't happened. But, Indonesia is buying American F-35s.

As the world goes into panic mode over a glorified common cold, death by economy will be greater than death by disease. People are afraid because people are afraid. Once they freak-out to full-freak capacity, they will look for someone to blame for all their fear. That takes us to China.

China doesn't like being the villain of the world. The Chinese Communist Party doesn't like looking bad. Who does? Most of that bad image throughout the world—including among the Chinese people themselves—comes from unedited videos of what the Chinese Communist government is doing to its own citizens. Other than uncut videos, people are irritated by reports of signs of organ harvesting along with appointing Communist Party bosses to new leadership positions also hurts China's image, both foreign and domestic.

Then, China blames the US Army—not the military, not the Marines, Navy, Air Force, nor Space Force, and not something more sensible like CIA. A Chinese official said that the US Army took the virus to China. A video is going viral in East Asia of Congressman Harley Rouda at a House Oversight Committee hearing questioning CDC Director Dr. Robert Redfield, "So, we could have people in the United States dying from what appears to be influenza, when in fact it could be the coronavirus or COVOID-19?" to which the director responds, "Some cases have been actually diagnosed that way in the United States to date." And, this is being used in China, and even among the Taiwanese, to argue that the pneumoniavirus existed in the United States long ago, wasn't noticed because it was misdiagnosed long ago, but the US Army then took the virus to China. Chinese speakers easily misunderstand because they don't know how democracy works. They believe this proves the pneumoniavirus originated in the US, even though there haven't been any epidemics of death-by-pneumonia in the US since the bacterial pneumonia epidemic of 1918.

As things progress, China is being pushed to the point of acting on an ancient psychotic belief that all of China's problems exist because China doesn't control Taiwan. If the Chinese PLA military attacks Taiwan, however, they won't be strong enough to deal with their own dissent at home. If China

doesn't invade Taiwan, it is because the
Communist Party has been rendered catatonic, not
knowing what to do.

Encore of Revival: America, March 23

Revival has returned. It's not in the streets yet and evil hasn't fled. But, revival has landed and is making its way across the country. Chicago rings church bells five times a day. Everywhere, Americans look up and ask whether God is trying to get our attention.

Duh.

As they were once called in the 80s, the "Kansas City Prophets" always said that God's judgments are merely intended to help us love more. Pain removes everything that limits our capacity to love and receive love. When crisis hits, we examine our priorities and look deep inside, hoping to have the one thing that matters most. And, we find it in our hearts. Of all the things we gain and lose in the world, the one thing we hope to have when everything else is shaken is our ability to still love. Once we find that we still have that ability, no matter how small, we feel like the richest in the world, having remembered that truly, all that matters is love.

Revival has returned.

The Communist Chinese thought that by refusing to supply America with pharmaceutical ingredients, panic would spread across America.

But, they were as wrong as the Grinch who thought he could steal Christmas from Whoville.

As crisis rises, not from a virus as much as our overreaction to it, America is returning in full swing to its core. Maybe we'll learn to ditch our drama. Maybe we'll learn a happy medium between our two favorite poles of fear and apathy. Even as we decide, small companies and neighbors are helping each other. We're seeing America at its best, just as it is during any time of crisis. We return to God, revival returns in return, and, like a giant rousing from its sleep once again, the American machine of love-in-crisis is in full swing.

Revival has returned.

Cadence of Conflict: Asia, March 23

China's in trouble—deep trouble. America pauses with the same hush of silence that swept the country from the outskirts of Washington to New Orleans in 1812, gathering around the radio in 1941, or staring at the same TV images on repeat in 2001. While America pauses and reflects, China accuses, taunts, and threatens, as if the world wasn't already angry enough about the jobs lost to a Communist country that promotes leaders for party loyalty rather than governing competence.

There is no PR campaign, no cooperation, no compensation that can buy back decades of ill will. That ill will against China was only fueled by governments and leaders who allowed themselves to be trodden on, quite an evil thing the West did to set China up for such embarrassment. But, the Communist Chinese do themselves no service by fitting the stereotype handed to them.

While China faces Western scorn, Taiwan shines like Venus at twilight. They have the breakout under control almost as much as they have public panic on mute. The Taiwanese premier jokes about everyone having only one butt hole, then encourages everyone to buy, buy, buy—it helps the economy, after all, and there is plenty of supply. While Taiwan clips right along, clamping down as needed, China's jealousy only simmers and froths. The Communists across the Straight want the results of capitalism and competence, without any of the actions or guiding virtues.

When scorn and jealousy mix and reach a critical boiling point, like fudge, China will start to harden. If these are the days when China invades Taiwan, a roused and ready America won't be the only thing stopping them. Taiwanese are already well-stocked at home from a virus that China perceivedly caused. They can stay at home. They have the defenses and pantries to hold out for America, who is alive and well and hungry to kick someone's butt.

Encore of Revival: America, March 30

The main cause of destruction in America is fear. The disease behind the panic is lack of manufacturing infrastructure.

For decades, America closed its factories, complained about lost jobs, then complained even more about prices being 5 cents too high. This made China rich. And, like the valedictorian-become-CEO who couldn't found a company to save his lunch, China was given wealth without the character-building experience to appreciate it. The Chinese got a big head, they stayed just as careless and abusive with law and order, things got out of hand, and now they are facing blame for not managing a virus they might not have even caused. That virus returned to its pontificated origin: the US. Unable to balance themselves between the poles of apathy and panic, Americans gave into fear, then fear of the virus—not the virus itself—wreaked havoc.

The virus alone was not enough to destabilize America. We needed two ingredients: a bipolar mindset of only-apathy vs only-panic and the closure of our manufacturing sector. Our lack of factories mixed our lack of mindful awareness reached critical mass with the virus serving as the spark that went boom.

Now, as Federal and State governments jockey for control of emergency supply chains, and the Federal government plays "Trump" cards (pun intended), America is addressing the two-time single cause of the problem. We are getting our factories rebuilt.

But, as Americans fear power grabs from the Federal government, and as the States appear to be the victims, an unintended consequence will erupt for anyone with a globalist agenda. The people will not only demand that factories be rebuilt; they will also demand that more powers be given to the States.

Cadence of Conflict: Asia, March 30

Blame! Both general theories about where this virus originated fail to do two things: They don't acquit anyone and they don't tell us how to treat it. The theories no longer seem to matter since fear has taken over the world.

Initially, we had a theory that the virus passed from wildlife to humans at a kind of so-called exotic meat market in Wuhan, a city in China. Then, a Chinese government official—later seen as a lone wolf not speaking for the pack—blamed the US Army specifically, as opposed to the US Military or CIA as the usual conspiracy theory suspects go. We'll look at the Army's place in Chinese politics later.

Upon review, there is a convincing case that the 2019-nCoV had its origin at a military laboratory and got out into the American public last summer before the CDC shut down that laboratory. But, this still doesn't explain how it would have gotten to Wuhan. And, both China and the US still face scorn for coverups and delayed response.

Then, we have China's negative PR campaign, two actually. Blaming the US "Army" feeds Chinese kook theory because the Chinese military is called the "Army". Even China's Navy is called the "People's Liberation Army Navy". It seemed from the outset as intended to tip Chinese cultural sentiment against America, not intending to be based in fact. Now, a few weeks later, the Chinese people fear "foreigners" (Westerners and 'Black People'). Old Chinese superstition still lingers, that Black People are cursed by the gods or by nature because black is the bad color in their culture.

As anti-foreign sentiment grows in China, the world grows more irritated with China. And, as the WHO digs its heels in on keeping Taiwan out, the world sees China controlling too much of the world through its deep pockets—a concern the international finance community had brought up from an article from Harvard Business Review, *How Much Money Does the World Owe China?*. When a WHO official hung up on an interview twice, we see that Harvard's curiosity wasn't irrelevant.

The world is responding in hatred toward China with such venom, people beat up Asians of any nationality, even those without any connection to China. Yes, the world propped up China for a grand fall into global disfavor. But, China still hasn't done anything to help itself. One little virus, no matter where it came from, was all it took to push the world over the brink.

Encore of Revival: America, April 6

Conspiracy theories fly. That's to be expected when the whole world is told to stay home. Some say 5G is the killer. Though suspicious as interesting, that doesn't explain everything. The more disturbing part is that the video was censored by Facebook and, reportedly, YouTube. Elsewhere, people are reporting empty hospitals around the world, contrary to reports by big news media. Most disturbing of all was the decision for governors to close schools, which runs against common sense. Consider an article published by AAPS* in which a doctor from Cadillac, Michigan explains that keeping schools open would have had the best affect on containment.

Public panic and shutting down the economy by closing the schools that would have slowed viral spread aside, look how the greater damage from overreacting is helping in other ways.

Trump only grows in popularity. Michigan's governor is in the spotlight and will be a likely pick for a typical establishment Democratic VP candidate come November. If she runs, the voters in Michigan she unemployed may vote against her in the general election. If that happens, she would likely be a one-term governor, facing a double loss like Scott Walker did after he lost in the 2016 presidential primaries.

More importantly, unexpected things are shifting. Businesses are forced to reinvent. While the masses go into panic mode, money is moving toward those who keep calm and level heads.

*https://aapsonline.org/cornoavirus-covid-19-public-health-apocalypse-or-panic-hoax-and-anti-american/

Cadence of Conflict: Asia, April 6

The pneumoniavirus is having a detrimental effect on China. While Xi Jinping kicks China's economy into full swing, the rest of the world is on full alert. Manufacturing moves home—whether to or from China. Countries seek alternate supply sourcing. Taiwan shines like a star of brilliance, set up as if to shame China by design. China's big mistake was going along with feeling shamed, as if by design. China could have played its hand with Taiwan the way the UK did with the American Revolution— claiming it lost a few colonies, but that it didn't matter. By pretending not to care, the world might not care and China would be unstoppable. Instead, China is taking every step possible to create new enemies and make old enemies worry.

In that wake, Taiwan grows in military and respect, even donating medical masks to other countries. The WHO now faces shame and doubt because of an evermore apparent bias toward China. Australia cooperates with the US in efforts to confront China. Critical voices in China are silenced or otherwise go missing. An employee of Hong Kong CEO Carrie Lam resigned, then killed himself. Kim Jong-Un makes more threats. East Asia is more volatile than ever. Times like these are what some call an "opportunity".

Encore of Revival: America, April 13

In America, many WWII measures are being reenacted and reutilized—fireside chats, not from the president, but from governors, massive government spending packages, unemployment, sporadic activity in the stock market, groceries in short supply, and, not least of all, hatred for an Asian country. This time, it's not "the Japs" (as the news called them), but "the Chinese".

While Democrats act like Democrats, Republicans act like Republicans. The president wants everyone to go back to work, Republicans talk about civil rights and freedom of gathering for religion, Democrats want money, big government, and fewer Christian gatherings in particular.

Then, we have citizen reports from around the world of empty hospitals reported on the news as overflowing "war zones". While conspiracy kooks claim the end of the world, this activity indicates more of a "virus drill", much like a "fire drill". Governments should run a kind of drill to see how to respond to a real pandemic. Of course, being semi-secret and all, Democrats and Republicans won't tell on each other, but they'll still try to push their partisan agendas. Leave it to a politician to capitalize on a fire drill.

But, that's what everyone does, right? Salesmen send free medical masks to prospective customers to break the ice. Companies offer their reinvented services, supposedly to "help with the situation". And, not least of all, while the world wakes up to need of domestic manufacturing, many countries are opening and reopening factories to make stuff at home once again. That's yet another WWII measure being reenacted.

Cadence of Conflict: Asia, April 13

The global case against China is marching forward in force. Typically the West doesn't care about human rights violations—they care, but never enough to do anything until it involves themselves. Two million Uyghurs missing in Xinjiang doesn't matter to the West. But, if Americans and Europeans are afraid of catching a pneumonia-cold that most people don't know anyone who died from, but they have to stay home without toilet paper—well, now it's time for a war. Who do the papers blame?—China.

Anti-Chinese sentiment is no joke. Taiwan is being painted as a key victim. The Chinese Communists are being labeled as the perpetrators of the global pandemic. Even in Israel, even among the anti-Trump American electorate, China is the biggest bad guy ever!

We can argue that China deserves it. We can argue that the West set up China by making China rich in the first place, then causing a fake pandemic. However we chalk it up, the West is coming for China. The saddest part of all comes from the Chinese.

A reporter working for a news company owned by a Chinese general makes a Chinese propaganda speech when "asking a question" to the president.

Chinese college students at Western schools march, protest, and even bully, all inline with Chinese Communist propaganda. And, while the West amasses force against China, the Chinese Communists only dig their heels in and feed the forest fire of hate raging against themselves.

Encore of Revival: America, April 20

The pneumoniavirus's biggest casualty is Democratic politics. As the party of ostensibly "helping people", Democratic governors gambled that "taking action" would sway public opinion in their direction. Michigan, Minnesota, and Virginia governors did not need to create the greatest restrictions among the States. But, their Democratic Party's moral compass guided them there. They might have added a dose or two of theatrics—especially understandable when one is in the DNC spotlight for the VP candidacy; clear your throat while saying, "Michigan."

It is a fascinating turn of the usual pendulum: States stepping on Constitutional rights while the Federal government defends them, all the while, States calling for more Federal powers while they object to the Federal powers stopping them.

The other factor is kookery. Since when did young Democratic voters, especially Sanders supporters, trust numbers put out by a Republican-controlled Federal government? Requirements for deciding "cause of death" do not include a diagnosis of disease, yet a disease is being declared the cause of death for many who have not been diagnosed. Those numbers come from a Republican-controlled Federal government, then Democratic voters enshrine those numbers to support Democratic governors' action.

What numbers are made-up and what is real remains another question that can't be answered now. The big takeaway is a meltdown in the Democratic voter base. Their justification of numbers doesn't make sense, nor does their idea that steps toward martial law will be popular. We could be looking at an even greater, greater Republican victory this November. That's interesting since the reported number of pneumoniavirus deaths hasn't come close to the number of abortions.

Cadence of Conflict: Asia, April 20

Just when we thought China couldn't make itself more unpopular, China made itself more unpopular. Perhaps it was charity. Perhaps it was delusion. We don't like thinking bad things about others, especially if we sacrificed our jobs and economies to have our stuff made more cheaply by them. Saying bad things about China was as politically incorrect as blaming the Karan for militants wanting to kill their enemies. Thinking bad things about China made Americans feel almost as guilty as thinking that voting against Obama wasn't racist. No one wanted to say that China might be up to no good.

Why governments and global economy jockeys supposedly didn't see it coming remains unexplained. But, all of a sudden, China is global enemy number one. The Western press has been educating the world about Taiwan in almost every Taiwan news story for the past decade. Anybody who is anybody at least asks, "What's the relationship between China and Taiwan?" To Western taxpayers and voters, no acceptable answer will be in China's favor. These days, China is damned if it does and more damned if it isn't.

Governments are paying factories to dump China's manufacturing. But, that's not the biggest problem for the Chinese.

No one gives as much money to the World Health Organization as the US, behind that is Bill Gates, then the UK. China is among the smallest donors. So, why is so much Western money being used along the propaganda points of such a puny donor as China? If so much money is being usurped, the US would be obligated to pull the plug. And, that's what it looks like, especially with the WHO siding with China on the matter of Taiwan. While Taiwan's exclusion from the WHO indicates bias, Western countries are concerned about the WHO helping cover up what happened in China.

With president Trump now calling for investigations in China about the pneumoniavirus, other problems could come up, such as the Uyghurs in Xinjiang. China won't allow that, not even to regain control of all that US money in the WHO. The world won't have it. Global hatred toward China is only beginning.

Encore of Revival: America, April 27

America is under a failing attack from Regressive Feudalism. They have been called "progressives", but with the economic pandemic caused by Democrats in State governments responding to a controversial virus, we now know their true goal. They don't represent all Democrats—such as the public-funding-minded Democratic voters. Specifically the "progressive Liberals" have not been seen until now for the "Regressive Feudalists" they actually are. This includes many Democrats in power, along with the under-40 Democratic voters who support so-called "SJWs" and "snowflake" activists.

It's failing, the attack. While a sometimes-seen-as "fake virus" took center stage, the Regressive Feudalists saw their opportunity. They couldn't resist confining each serf to a manor. Enter Michigan Governor Gretchen "Witless" Whitmer. For her valiantly failed attempted return to feudalism, she likely cooked her own goose twice. As the hero to the Regressives, she may have earned her vice presidential candidacy with Joe Biden, who can't win, along with having sealed her own fate as a one-term governor.

Regressive Feudalism has permanently failed because it tried to assert itself at a time and in a

way that damaged the economy. As Clinton years
wisdom says, "It's the economy, stupid."
Republicans in the Federal government have been
calling for a lift on the bans, so those Republicans
will claim the economic results, which will sway
the election.

But, failure never stopped Regressives before. This
time, an opinion writer in the New York Times has
twisted the harmless nature of the controversial
pneumoniavirus into a call for targeting people
with no symptoms. If many, many, many people
have the virus, but don't have symptoms, then the
virus must not be as bad as it is purported. But,
with the Regressive worldview that everyone is a
pathetic serf in need of protection from the Holy
government establishment, even good news is a
reason to panic.

Just the same, Sky News finally stopped hiding
reports of empty hospitals after weeks of global
media censorship and deleted Facebook and
YouTube videos. Their spin: Empty hospitals prove
that everyone is in more danger of a virus that is
so dangerous that most people will never know
they had it.

Somehow, all good news chalks up to all bad news
for the Regressive Feudalists, now on the march.
Make no mistake: They will fail just as surely as
they will keep marching anyway. They want to
fight; that's why they are Feudalists.

Cadence of Conflict: Asia, April 27

China is under global attack from all sides. It's not just the government, but a sizeable portion of the Chinese people who cooperate with that government. We don't know how many in China are part of the problem or the solution. Reports from China remain silenced and Chinese culture is beaten down and overtly compliant even to tyranny. While Chinese students at Western universities volunteer themselves as mouthpieces for Chinese Communist propaganda, they join the party deemed guilty by the jury of the world.

African governments are in panic about Chinese government gentrification of their own nations. China is seen as the villain who covered up information vital to the EU. Great Britain is fed up with China, claiming the Chinese don't just lack or hide information, but lie about it. Trump has been warning the world about China since before he was president—arguably that got him elected.

Then again, there's Taiwan again. Former US ambassador to the UN, Nikki Haley, has a petition for Taiwan to be admitted to the WHO. Even in a recent scuffle over some infected Navy sailors who walked around in Taiwanese public, there still are no new person-to-person virus cases in Taiwan 14 days later. The staggering success is largely accredited to Taiwan's miraculously brilliant and swift handling of the situation. It's all based on a germ-phobic population, slow and steady sectional school closing protocols, but it started with immediate and utter lockdown against the since-become world villain: China.

Taiwan has foresight. Maybe that's why China wants Taiwan out of the WHO. And now, the truth isn't hiding anymore.

Encore of Revival: America, May 4

America is furious, both of them. Conservatives are fed up with restrictions against a virus that has no symptoms. Liberals are fed up with Conservatives not entering panic mode with them.

If you don't believe in God, you will believe in anything. For some, it is the belief that animals will live as if forever if we are all vegetarian. For some, it is the belief that crashing economies and avoiding other humans is the only way to survive. For some, it is the belief that outbursts of rage are the only way to become happy.

Neither of the Americas seem willing to give up their respective beliefs in whatever they hold most dear. The only changes are the removal of ambiguity and the level of rage that follows. There is no "moderate" politician anymore. There is no "gray", only monochrome vision which will only find a way to gain evermore stark contrast.

They myth of people with different ideals living side-by-side is debunked. Maybe some ideals can live in a mixed society with one person living next to a neighbor who disagrees without being disagreeable; but not with Liberals and Conservatives. It's not that the Conservatives don't want it, but the Liberals won't allow it.

Our different views must not mix, they can only be partitioned with Liberal in one city and Conservative in another. That's the only way forward and it will happen because both will become too extreme for the other.

Cadence of Conflict: Asia, May 4

The anti-China machine is in full gear. Western nations are cranking out new reasons to hate China every day. Some is true, some is not, all is justified because China chose to respond in control, concealment, and censorship. Much how George W Bush build a case against Iraq, which many believed to be fake from the get go, people will support action against China because of other indisputable things China has done.

The better road would have been to empower China with values rather than enabling China with money. Some foolishly thought, or at least claimed to think, that giving China Western money would teach China Western values. That's as silly an idea as thinking that giving a child a birthday cake every day will teach the child to appreciate hard work. Instead of virtue, the West raised China be like Marie Antoinette who answered poverty by saying, "Let them eat cake."

China's solution to Western growth is to defeat the West with technology copied from the West. That's not a nation that learned our values, but underappreciated our hard work to a point that they would go to war with great weakness: lack of ingenuity. Like a butcher prepares a cow, the West

fattened China for the slaughter and China was all
to happy to get fat and angry.

Encore of Revival: America, May 11

The difference between Tara Reade and Blasey Ford is tears. Justices Kavanaugh and Thomas also had tears. Then Senator Joe Biden chaired the committee at Clarence Thomas's hearing about harassing Anita Hill two just years before his alleged assault on Tara Reade. If the allegation is true, he knew better. And, according to Tara, his words did more damage than his hands.

The DNC can't drop Joe Biden. If DNC superdelegates overturn the favorite candidate of Democratic voters, their non-democratic methods would be exposed, just as their values already have. Remember, this is the party that supports and is supported by a promiscuous culture.

The Democratic Party has forced itself to own this. Conservative voters won't be swayed when Democrats throw Tara under the bus. Being the party of ostensibly defending the defenseless— being the party of women, minorities, and anti-harassment—ignoring such allegations would remove their platform and their platitudes with it. As with Democratic friends like Weinstein and others in Hollywood, compassion was but a show.

Being ignored, hated, and accused are similar feelings to things going on elsewhere. A nurse in New York tries to save patients from being killed in what seems like claims of medical malpractice. Dr. Judy Mikovits was threatened and pushed, jailed and gag ordered. The passive aggression is the same. The verbal abuse is the same. The ability for the bully to get under people's skin is the same. And, the self-destruction of the abusers, which always follows, is the same.

These stories of abuse are strikingly similar to the petty politics in power struggles in local church horror stories. A small pastor feels threatened, then starts talking down to parishioners, then entices heckling against anyone who wants to leave. Those who survived social abuse from institutional religion don't find anything surprising about the stories from Tara Reade or Judy Mikovits or a New York nurse.

If you want to know how this will play out, research the trend-setters who somehow find themselves ahead of the curve. Research what happens to controlling clergy vs Christians who discover that Jesus is alive and well outside of Sunday morning walls. That is exactly where America is headed.

Cadence of Conflict: Asia, May 11

China must brace itself for war. Regardless of any plot from America being true or false, how Beijing handled Wuhan—or rather mishandled—will not be overlooked by the free world. Regardless of how different governments handled the outbreak, the West will see an outbreak that wouldn't have happened if China had followed the same forthright standards that the West does. The West thought China was on its way to following standards. But, Confucian Communism knows no standard except its own authoritarianism.

How did China get this far? There is so much in China to be desired, including the Bible-based government Dr. Sun Yat-Sen started over a century ago. Chinese medicine addresses many matters of health that elude Western pharmacy. Politeness, indirection, family, and respect—these are virtues the West could have learned from China. Except, just look at what's happening now.

The term kowtow came from Hong Kong Cantonese. Bowing and placating the bully emboldens the bully. For all their virtues, China was crushed by its Confucian insistence of monolithic thinking—that there is only one idea: the idea you are told to have—that hypotheticals do not exist because everyone only considers the idea we are all told to promote. When a people are beaten down and trained to beat each other down to train each other so, that people's leaders will think they can get away with anything. China was even placated by Western trade and tech. Christian pastors in China who wouldn't drop their Confucianism were placated by Western seminaries. The West emboldened the dragon. Lo, Beijing today!

War follows a schedule of logistics. The West doesn't want China's military to get any bigger. Taxpayers in the West are learning about the "plandemic" roots of the virus China neglected into going global. Public rage against China won't build forever. The great Western provocation must happen before the people lose interest. That is China's greatest threat: time.

Encore of Revival: America, May 18

Democrats are in full-swing takeover mode and they aren't sneaking past anyone. Their Regressive-Feudalist base knows it and supports it. The Conservatives know it. Trump knows it. It is an act of desperation from the Democratic Party machine that seeks permanently-dependent classes—and now, apparently, permanently-dependent States.

Polls argue that Trump is ahead in Michigan. But, Michigan residents will likely blame Michigan's current disaster on Gretchen "Whitless" Whitmer, who is the Democratic VP Nominee Apparent. Biden needs her from such a battleground because he doesn't stand a chance any other way.

The word is out about Bill Gates's plans for depopulation—AKA mass genocide. Germans have had enough of uneeded lockdowns. One man held a sign adopted from the Tarantino film "Kill Bill" overlayed with a picture of the Microsoft Bill. The public will not go quietly into the night. Americans who oppose the lockdowns are by no means alone.

While Pelosi seeks to change election rules to accommodate for a virus, she clearly hopes to push this current crisis through November. Democrats are throwing a tantrum in the presence of a strong and growing Conservative base. This is making new converts who don't like the chaos that the Left wants to snowball. Don't hold your breath for a Democrat-led November. The lie that Democrats just want to help people has been seen for what it is: Democrats want to make people need to be helped by them.

Cadence of Conflict: Asia, May 18

It was a week of slap after slap in China's face. Congress pokes at Human Rights in Xinjiang among other old-news grievances. China "warns" the US—again—about Huawei, apparently unaware that warnings require power or at least clout, of which China retains neither.

As blame circulates against China for a global outbreak, Taiwan courts favor. Airlines have corrected a listing that identifies Taiwan as somehow part of China or something-or-other. You know you've lost when airline companies aren't even afraid of you.

The dirtiest and best-kept secret is about war. China can't even threaten military action against America because of the elections in America. While American polling likely lies as usual, war is good for any sitting president's numbers. Threat of war would be good news for America's incumbent, whomever that incumbent may be.

So, China is left with a choice: Wait until the West is even stronger in China's back yard and face shame for not acting or else respond to Western provocation to start a war too early and face shame for losing. All China has to go on is persistent delusions of ancient grandeur. We'll see how that works out.

Encore of Revival: America, May 25

The Left's reckoning is on its way. Many police officers in many states and counties refuse to enforce lockdown orders from governors. It may seem that the reckoning is already here, but we haven't reached November yet.

While Democratic governors irritate and aggravate the public—thinking it will stir victory in November—some voters may be throwing in the towel. The DNC and mainstream news narrative was that "Trump stole the election". Democratic voters may be statistically inclined to believe what government and news say, but they are not as stupid as the DNC thinks they are. If Trump stole the election, some might think there is no point in voting in the next election.

Then, there are pneumoniavirus death rates. The Guardian reports that three times as many Black people died as White. If that were true—considering that the DNC prides itself as the party for minorities—that means Democrats lost voters. With Democratic governors and their lockdown orders not having saved Black lives that matter, why would remaining Blacks continue to support Democrats? If indeed "medical murder" were involved as some have claimed... Let's just say that the more stories that get uncovered, the more it

looks like the Democratic Party-news cartel only
hurts itself as the only solution to hurting itself.

Then there are lies, then darn lies, then statistics.
The press cartel often uses reporting and polling to
sway public opinion. But, they make sure to
include a few last-page "could-be" stories so that
when their false reporting doesn't change the
election outcome as they wanted, they can still
claim that they are credible news sources. Harry
Enten* at CNN looked over polling** history of
presidential re-election years and found
correlations to other re-elected presidents,
suggesting that—silent on the matter of
Democratic governors having gained such public
trust—there is a chance that Trump could be on a
pathway to re-election. Ya think?

*https://edition.cnn.com/profiles/harry-enten

**https://edition.cnn.com/2020/05/20/politics/
trump-2020-analysis/index.html

Cadence of Conflict: Asia, May 25

Taiwan has a new Vice President: Former Premier William Lai, known for his pro-independence posture. China won't be happy, but China is rarely happy these days.

The Chinese made two loud omissions in their rhetoric this week. When talking about reunification with Taiwan, they left out the word "peaceful". The press noticed. A Taiwan official said it meant the same thing. But, everyone knew better because China also left out regard for Hong Kong's Basic Law, something else that always got mentioned in the past.

Apparently, Beijing thinks peace and honoring treaties are too petty to be bothered with.

But, certain terms are in need of clarity. Xi Jinping isn't merely trying to "reunify with Taiwan"; his actions are closest to that of a corporate hostile takeover—not just of Taiwan, but the entire world.

In Australia, Drew Pavlou faces expulsion from Queensland University for organizing student protests in support of Hong Kong opposition to recent law proposals, especially extradition to China and the recent "security" proposal. Follow the money. Australia's government is looking into China's influence. Many other governments are too.

According to the *Hong Kong Human Rights and Democracy Act**, US Congress is required to review whether Hong Kong is autonomous enough to have its visas treated separately from the rest of China. Secretary of State Mike Pompeo is already late in his report. He waited until China held its own congress meetings. What happened at those meetings didn't help the case for Hong Kong's autonomy.

**https://en.wikipedia.org/wiki/ Hong_Kong_Human_Rights_and_Democracy_Act*

Encore of Revival: America, June 1

It's amazing what can happen in a week. It's amazing what a week can reveal about what quietly happened over the course of decades. America has somehow attracted and cultivated a police force with an attitude other than one "to serve and protect".

Minnesota and Minneapolis are run by Democrats. So are New York and New York. Neighborhoods with violent rioting over the abominable murder of George Floyd see violent responses from more abominable police. What we see from police against all demographics of protesters makes Hong Kong look gentle. It's atrocious how provocative police are seen in footage coming from the protests.

As Will Smith said, "Racism is not getting worse, it's getting filmed." So is police disregard for the public.

America has a systemic racism problem compounded with a supremacist police problem. These days, people don't consciously disdain others for skin color—not much. Instead, we accept certain events as part of the narrative. If a White pastor mugs someone, that's headline news. If a Black man gets killed by a cop, oh well tragedies happen all the time. Thanks to what little freedom is left in social media, we got to see just how unabashed murderous cops have become. When they killed George Floyd, it seemed routine.

With politicians the saying goes, "Not all are bad; it's just the 99% that give a bad rap for the rest of them."

Yeah, the bad apples give the bushel a bad name. Many police out there really do want to make a positive change, to repair what we have come to accept and expect. But, there are a lot more bad apples than the public narrative gave credit to. It seems that good apples gave too good a rap to a half-rotten bushel. At least now we know.

Cadence of Conflict: Asia, June 1

China says every effort will be made for peaceful reunification with Taiwan as long as there remains hope; force is the last resort. But, Taiwan wants peaceful freedom from tyranny; force is the last resort. There is no hope for China to find any reunification with Taiwan of any kind. China has removed any desire for peaceful reunification with it's pressured propaganda campaigns around the world and in Taiwan, not to mention terrible handling of Hong Kong. Taiwan has prevented any hope of forceful reunification by arming to the teeth in response to China's backfired PR campaigns.

Taking Taiwan would hurt and cost both lives and resources. And, Russia knows this. With steep cliffs on the east coast, complex deltas plains on the west coast, and a capital city inside a mountain bowl at the north, any beach landing would make Normandy Beach look like a walk in the park. With mountains peaking even higher than Fuji, China faces a jungle battle like halted America in Vietnam, except this battle would only be uphill.

If China prioritized such a venture, using either or both of its two copied aircraft carriers with its copied fighter jets and its copied missiles and copied drones, China's neighbors would see an opportunity even if the US didn't respond with any of its forty-four home-made carriers.

India, with one billion people, is no forced-friend of China, especially in recent months. A Taiwan distraction would be the perfect chance to free Tibet. Two thousand years of anti-friendship relations between Vietnam and China would require enormous numbers of soldiers to keep the Vietnamese from taking Nanjing as a pathway to the island of Hainan. Vietnam has a motive anyway, keep China at a safer distance for its history of aggression. With China occupied at the west and east while squandering enormous forces at Taiwan, Japan—a larger economy than India—has its own grudge and would love the chance for target practice near Beijing. None of the other countries small enough to be bought off and bullied would bring much help nor will to China's aid.

Then, there's the US after China would be in enough trouble. Russia doesn't want more trouble, for all Moscow's effort to seduce Europe by appearing pacifist. If China ever did manage to reach a Pyrrhic victory over Taiwan, China would have no defenses left, Tibet might be gone, then Japan and Vietnam would have taken their own bits out of the map. China would be clean pickings between the US and China's frenemy Russia.

Russia is no friend of China. Who do you think gave China the idea of this wasted pursuit? All of that assumes things go well with the one billion Chinese who hate their government more than ever before in history.

So, why did Taiwan request a lower-grade missile— because it comes with a vehicle Taiwan already has? It's not because Taiwan actually needs it. No. Talking about arming again to the teeth already armed to puts a kind of social pressure on Beijing, a sense of urgency. Taiwan sees what China is up against. Taiwan knows that Confucian culture can't pass up the opportunity to self-destruct in order to save face. Taiwan's policy is clear: Bring it.

Encore of Revival: America, June 8

As if shutting down for a virus weren't enough, the police just had to keep up old, bad, dirty habits. Few people question the reasoning behind vandalizing buildings when needed change hasn't happened. Floyd was killed in a Democratic district. Los Angeles and New York are Democratic districts. Republican and Democratic voters are equally irked; both believe not changing their vote this November is the way to make the needed change, except that Minneapolis seems bound to get a different mayor, which doesn't leave many party options. Through the partisan divide, other shady things have happened.

Reports of vandals being from out of town smell like rent-a-mob mischief. A construction site just happened to have an unattended pile of bricks, which just happened to be used to destroy the building across the street? Protests must be heard, just as fake protests must be investigated to find out whatever truth tells. At the end of it all, we are likely to find mischief both real and fake.

Dirty cops should be blamed for buildings destroyed. Dirty cops should be blamed for giving rent-a-mobs an excuse. And, dirty cops must be shut down, people are fed up and have been for a long time.

The country will carry on. Peaceful and fair people
who look after their neighbors will shine during
these times. Those who harbor blame and rage
won't be able to contain it, they won't even be able
to function. The election will most likely continue
on schedule. Rioting will only make it harder for
Democratic districts to vote and injustice will only
make it harder for Democrats to win re-election.
We all face a choice.

Cadence of Conflict: Asia, June 8

If The Chinese think poll numbers looking low or that the unrest in America means the Xi doctrine has a widening path on the road ahead, they should think again. But, being Confucian Communist, that's hard.

Trump actually may be ahead of where he was when he ran against Hillary. And, if the one president who could stand up to China were really on the outs, the last thing America's government would want is for the news media to report on it. It's a rouse. America and Trump are far better positioned to take on China than anti-society new media would have us think.

Mayor Han of Kaohsiung in Taiwan just faced a recall election and he got spanked. In a vote of 939k to 25k, the China hopeful from the grand old KMT-Nationalist Party faced a humiliation that the rest of the party might never overcome. The Kaohsiung city council speaker reportedly jumped to his death. Mayor Han had challenged Taiwan's president in the general election and lost, now his own constituency dumped him. It wasn't just a reprisal on him or his party; it was a reprisal against China. He ran on a platform of reuniting with China. These days, China is unpopular because of decisions within China's power to change.

Hong Kong is another hot spot for bad press. While Hong Kong could never stop China alone, Hong Kongers have been a platform on which China showed the world how China does things. And, the world isn't having it.

We're past the point of common sense and diplomatic shuffles. Nothing China even could do ever would change anyone's opinion. The world already has its mind made up.

Encore of Revival: America, June 15

America faces a new kind of reconciliation. Democrat voters in Seattle have decided that government can be overbearing. Usually, that was a patent held by Republican-voting Conservatives. A group of citizens expected the government to obey their desires, another idea Conservatives faced opposition for. And, the news media falsely claims that this group in Seattle wants to become a separate nation and erase all borders. Usually, slander from the media was an honor reserved for Conservatives.

Things have reversed.

If a group of people have bad beliefs, the best way to survive those beliefs is to have those beliefs known so they can be rebutted fair and square. Listening is a vital part of proving someone wrong. The nation has a lot of growing up to do.

Democrat voters and Republican voters hold this in common more now than ever: refusal to listen. Republican voters believe that if a group in Seattle has an opinion, they are automatically wrong and therefore shouldn't be heard nor should any claim of what they say be confirmed. Likewise, Democrat voters think if Trump says something, he is automatically wrong and anyone who says otherwise should be ignored without checking facts.

We have much more in common than we thought. But, the mutual refusal to listen tells us that fighting will only increase. Peace only comes to those who want it. Perhaps, the troubles our voluntarily deaf ears create will drive us to want to not fight more than we want to not listen—maybe.

Cadence of Conflict: Asia, June 15

The West and China just won't back down from each other. China will no longer try to work through former Mayor Han of Kaohsiung to reunite Taiwan against the will of 23 million people. America wants to put new missiles in China's back yard and every ally has turned down the offer except Taiwan, who hasn't had the chance. Australia is putting out the word on China, it's not the best place to study and coercion won't work. Now, North Korea is selling sand—illegally, of course, since selling anything has been deemed "illegal" by the West.

The sad part about the predictability of this conflict is how many were surprised by it. China never wanted to Westernize, otherwise it wouldn't have injected so many "Confucian" centers to indoctrinate other countries with their ancient Chinese ideals. All those students and propagandists from China were welcomed to teach Chinese or learn from the West, but when their Confucian-Communist colors shown, it all unraveled in a flash. Both professors and businesses that received Chinese money are sent packing.

But, we were always headed here. When ideological differences spread too broad, irreconcilable

differences are destined to break whatever
scaffolding temporarily binds us together. To those
who saw it, they haven't been affected by the
divide. For the rest, the damage hurts to much not
to blame and rage. And, that will only build.

Encore of Revival: America, June 22

The Left is desperate and the Right is getting even moreso. With Chief Justice Roberts casting the deciding vote with Liberal justices, kicking back Trump's move against DACA, Trumpists will lean in more than ever to fill upcoming Clinton-appointed vacancies with Conservatives.

Why would a million people reserve seats for a rally, then not show? Tump's Tulsa rally seemed small, but there was more going on. Democrat-voting "influencers" are reported to have mocked the event—an act of desperation. How did they know? One doesn't need to chide a president who is losing on his own. The social media platform TikTok was also reported involved—another act of desperation, and they are owned by the Chinese.

Surprisingly low turnouts are rare for Trump events. Mischief from the Left is suspect, squatter reservations and virus lock down policies among them. Low-turnout Tulsa won't be overlooked in the Trump chronicles. And, it will rouse Republican voters while setting Democratic voters at ease to think the election is stacked in Biden's favor.

While state and city police deal with protests, Trump steps back to allow local governments to work, yet he introduced some of the most sweeping police reform policy ever. Congress also is pushing for police reform.

As the looming election casts its normal shadow of question and concern, we are finally forced to deal with old problems which never should have been, just as much as no one found a way to escape them, let alone end them—until now.

Cadence of Conflict: Asia, June 22

China seems desperate for war. America has typically been the infamous provocateur. That's how China paints things. That's how Japan and Germany saw things. But, China has taken up a new role.

Buzzing jets into Taiwanese airspace is just one concern. China also sends fishing boats to ram Taiwan's Coast Guard and sand ships just to annoy. These won't convince the Taiwanese that China's rule would be preferable to status quo. Taiwanese respond by demanding more money for military and more weapons purchases from America.

Hong Kong looks grim as Beijing closes its stranglehold. There's no question anymore whether China held up its end of the bargain on its treaty that allowed Hong Kong to return. The question is whether anyone in the West cares. Hong Kongers have done all they can.

Meanwhile, Trump hasn't forgotten. In America's election, China "trumps" many topics, as it were—including the economy, the virus, Biden's past, and even war. The only reason China hasn't stepped up its aggression is unawareness: China doesn't know how American elections work because China doesn't understand the concept of democracy, as

Hong Kong's deterioration shows. To those who know, Trump faces a statistically likely victory. Holding out for November might prove too late.

Encore of Revival: America, June 29

And then, the TV numbers came in.

Trump's low-turnout rally in Tulsa melted down the media. 8 million viewers on Fox News eclipsed some 2 million on rival networks CNN and MSNBC. It was the highest-rated Saturday night for Fox News ever and, with advertisers, it was the most valued. Numbers don't lie.

This supposed "White power" retirement rally in Florida is a rouse. The man's words were sarcastic, as a provocative, comical comeback against some venomous parade trolls. At the pro-Trump golf cart procession, the anti-Trump crowd hawked and jeered. One lady jumped in front of an oncoming golf cart to force a collision, then demanded to see "the officer", who never showed, until her own peers pulled her back and let the man pass. He stuck out his tongue at her. What evil!

Adding to last week's list of reasons Trump will be reelected—mainly that he has neither defied campaign promises nor shown gross incompetence nor negligence—the opponent is boring. Joe Biden stirs the suspense of a sloth, much like Romney and McCain, whose lack of anything tellable successfully reelected Obama.

More than that, the anti-Trumpists seem histrionic. They don't show the overly-dramatized performance of a group that is not losing. There's more to proving a lack of minority support than someone convincingly saying, "Where are the minorities!?" But, anti-Trumpists don't think so. If, indeed, minorities didn't support Trump, those emphatic, emotional, convincing performances wouldn't be necessary. Over-done theater from the Left isn't the strongest cause for a Trump re-election, but it is the most convincing evidence this week.

Cadence of Conflict: Asia, June 29

At what point is it okay to bully the bad guy? At what point does bullying the bad guy make the bully the bigger bad guy? This is a line China is fast approaching and the US is fast leaving.

The thinking goes, "If you just did the good things I demand, then the great harm I did you in response wouldn't have happened." Of this, both China and America are guilty. That's why they are headed toward a conflict.

China pushes more and more toward this in the Far East while America brings home troops from previous venture wars in the Middle East. China is stepping-up bully responses while America backs off from them. But, both harbor that same "I'm allowed to do anything because I'm right" attitude. Both China and America need to repent. Perhaps God allowing this war will get some people there, or perhaps not. That choice is up to the individual.

Regardless of choice and attitude, we know things are only escalating. China passes a law grossly violating the 1984 treaty with Great Britain. That, technically, un-returns Hong Kong to China, though the wise, shrewd Crown hasn't said so yet. America has recognized this first, giving third-party credibility. If China's plan were to endear the world and win hearts with a show of its kindness,

it's failed. It's hard to show a kindness one does
have because it's hard to have kindness one
resents in favor of winning at any cost.

Encore of Revival: America, July 6

Happy Independence! Americans celebrated their declaration almost 250 years ago on Saturday. The country has coexisted with unseen freedoms in many ways and unheard deafness to its own oppression in others. It serves as a reminder that we live in a Republic only as long as we keep it. It's not the job of presidents nor judges nor legislators to preserve our freedoms for us.

Chief Justice Roberts made a decision that baffled some, but not those who remember his deciding vote on Obamacare. Arguably, having voted to keep Obamacare on the books was the bail of hay that broke the camel's back and elected Trump. Now, this election mover has stirred the electorate once again toward a choice that will move us closer to the inevitable reversal of Roe v. Wade.

As we approach "election solstice", the Left puts out every argument it can drum up to oppose Trump. It seems overdone for a group that claims to believe they will win November. And, they ignore deeper matters that move Trump votes.

Much more is at stake other than abortion. China is taking over with a force to eclipse Japan's expansion in the 1940s. No one was willing to not capitulate to China except Trump. If he were not re-elected, we might have no discussion on civil rights because the Chinese would be killing everyone in America who is not Han.

But then, America's military is spread too thin and neither Republican nor Democratic president has worked to reduce our expanding global presence, none except Trump. There's also the matter of manufacturing and closing the border to China over a virus when Democrats wanted to keep it open.

While our nation is in no position to decide an election on the social issues when basic needs are at stake, we are thankfully forced to address our neglected past. Intolerance over the atrocities of racism won't shift the election because those lines have already been drawn. By not being distracted with yet another failed political solution to racial healing, we the People will actually have to deal with the wounds of racism ourselves. Maybe something will finally get done.

Cadence of Conflict: Asia, July 6

It's official. China has broken the treaty that allows Hong Kong to be Chinese. The last time Britain accused China of breaking treaty, the Royal Navy opened fire on the Taiwan city of Tainan in 1858. The time before that was just a few decades earlier, when Britain obtained Hong Kong Island in a surrender from the Chinese after the Opium Wars.

Those wars began because China believed it was fair for silver to flow out of Britain, but only tea leaves to flow out of China. China would not accept British inventions and technology in trade, only silver for leaves. Opium was another leaf, one some in China were willing to return silver to Britain in exchange for.

For China, friendship has always been a one-way street. The Opium Wars did not begin with British military intervention. They started with an unbalanced sense of justice from China and subversion in response from Britain. While the British military did not start the wars, it ended them.

Now, China has passed a law in Beijing that affects the streets of Hong Kong. That violates the 1984 Sino-British Joint Declaration, the basis for Hong Kong's return to China. It seems 150 years have not changed anyone's disposition. China wants

laws written in one city, then obeyed in another.
China wants to make promises, then ignore them.
Britain will not respond with military, but with
subversion. In the end, America's military may play
a role, but Hong Kong will likely return to the
British for one, single reason. History repeats for
those who refuse to learn from it.

Encore of Revival: America, July 13

In the Supreme Court ruling on Congress' subpoena of the president, everyone claims the ruling was in their favor. Democratic members of Congress point out the court's statement that one branch is not above the law. Trump points out the court's decision to return the pro-subpoena decision of a lower court decision as unfinished homework. The subpoena will not go into effect before the end of the session of Congress that ordered it. Trump is accused by the media of a meltdown for saying so and Democrats call their defunct subpoena a victory.

What in the Hill is going on? In the court's decision to return the incomplete ruling, Chief Justice Roberts briefly quoted Hamilton from *Federalist No. 71*. Consider a fuller quote:

> The representatives of the people, in a popular assembly, seem sometimes to fancy that they are the people themselves, and betray strong symptoms of impatience and disgust at the least sign of opposition from any other quarter; as if the exercise of its rights, by either the executive or judiciary, were a breach of their privilege and an outrage to their dignity. They often appear disposed to exert an imperious control over

the other departments; and as they commonly have the people on their side, they always act with such momentum as to make it very difficult for the other members of the government to maintain the balance of the Constitution.

This is a problem as ancient as legislatures themselves. Congress can't skip process when giving a subpoena, even to a president, anymore than one can be immune from a subpoena, even the president. Both tried, both failed, but only Congress lost something of substance. This Congress will end before a decision is reached and there will be no tax records shown before the election. Still, Congressional Democrats delusionally declared victory. What Hamilton described in Congress may be called "narcissistic rage" by psychologists today.

As seen in response to the pneumoniavirus, Democrats think that crippling the economy and forcing dependace on the State will boost their popularity. But, such measures wouldn't be needed if Democrats were as popular—and Trump were as unpopular—as the media touts them to be. Given their apparent view of the world, this makes perfect sense.

Neither party in Congress speaks for the worldview of any large portion of the people. Republicans in Congress are largely elitist; the vast majority of their voters are not. Democrats in Congress speak for a small segment of their own votership as well—

those few who are anti-life, who fear everything, whose action unchecked would kill everything, who nonetheless fear that anything could kill them, and who believe that everyone else thinks the same.

This is interesting because the psychological behavior of "projecting" one's own view onto others is a trait of Narcissistic Disorder. Thankfully, they are not the majority they think themselves to be, not even within their own party. It is ironic timing that psychology journals are reporting a condition being called "PTBO", where people who are easily offended are clinically proven less effective in the workplace. We don't need to say which political ideology the affected group of that study would likely fall into. Week by week, an ever greater majority of America wakes up to the insanity of Capitol Hill.

Cadence of Conflict: Asia, July 13

China and the US have shown their intentions to the world. The new "National Security Law", passed and interpreted solely by the Chinese Communist Party, applies to the entire world. China made it illegal for Americans to support calls for change in Hong Kong. Germans wearing a Winnie-the-Pooh shirt could be guilty of a Chinese crime against China's national security. This is no joke.

The US went hard line after China over Uyghurs in Xinjiang this week. 78 members of Congress petitioned President Trump from both parties to declare China's work with the Uyghurs "genocide". That is not merely rhetoric nor an attempt to insult, but a step to unlock later military permissions. The US is preparing for invasion, either to land US troops or to support some other military that does, such as India. This is no joke.

China clarified its understanding on two fronts.

Firstly, about Uyghurs in Xinjiang, China responded to America's visa sanction and frozen asset action against Chinese officials with a tit-for-tat policy. By not responding with military preparation, or at least genocide declaration, China misinterpreted what the US is ultimately preparing.

Secondly, Chinese state media have commented how the new "National Security Law" for Hong Kong would apply if China could assert jurisdiction elsewhere. This means that, just as the US is laying in the groundwork for an invasion of China, China is laying in the groundwork for what would follow an invasion anywhere else. In all likelihood, the US' response concerning Uyghurs in Xinjiang—paving a way for invasion—showed understanding of China's plans for invasion, less likely not, but surely the sabers have been unsheathed and are no longer just rattling.

Encore of Revival: America, July 20

America is facing a crisis. Powerful forces with big money pull the strings. Had they pulled the strings differently, the world might not be in the situation it is in. Look at the Gates Foundation funding of the World Health Organization. What kind of sway was squandered in that influence?

While an epidemic that seemed to be passing resurges, Democratic voters turn to government guidelines while Republican voters turn to the Republican party. People are distracted with solving the current crisis, in a strong struggle over how.

Meanwhile in Washington, Senator Biden toys with the idea of removing the Senate rule allowing the filibuster—that would require only 51 Senate votes for most laws to pass instead of 60. With Americans—from both sides of the political schism—turning to government to solve today's problems, a powerful Senate could become the most dangerous tool in the world.

As for Trump's re-election, we see a massive push from Left-leaning media to paint the election as a Republican failure. Their arguments are based on what is right and reasonable from a Left wing view. But, whether correct or a matter of opinion, elections aren't determined by what is right or wrong or reasonable; elections are determined by the popular vote. Right now, right or wrong, reported or ignored, Trump supporters are the majority.

We can't trust surveys to say otherwise because those surveys always forecast Republican failure around this time in every election year. No Republican victory was ever reported as anything other than a surprise by the media, not even Fox News in 2016. So, if a Republican victory looks like it would be a surprise, historically speaking, that only makes it all the more likely.

Biden's campaign is based on encouragement through difficult times and incompetence of the current president. His ads are long. Without difficult times or incompetence of the incumbent, Biden has no message. His appeals are akin to Jimmy Carter's in the election he lost.

Trump's campaign is built on his own competence, campaign promises he kept through laws, orders, and appointments, and resolve to continue pushing. His ads are short and sometimes censored on the internet.

The difference in the two campaigns, by itself, is enough to determine the outcome. As for the Democratic view that Trump was incompetent with the pneumoniavirus outbreak, Trump supporters blame Democratic politicians, Bill Gates, and China. They fear as much as Democratic voters, and they have their reason to keep their Republican vote unchanged. The epidemic doesn't change votes, it only increases how adamant voters are on not changing their votes.

Unlike Republican voters, Democrat voters know the issues to address, but they don't know how things happen in the world. So, the inevitable Trump victory in November will surprise them. Then, they will go into rage and possible riots. The Senate could grab for power as could China.

In tough times, people awaken. These are tough times. We will get through them. But, it won't be smooth sailing.

Cadence of Conflict: Asia, July 20

Hong Kong is seriously considering shutting itself down. Many may argue that Hong Kong is certainly shutting down, but a basic understanding of humanity says that people are resilient. China claims that doing whatever China wants inside Hong Kong is good, right, and fair, regardless of the promise not to do so until 2047. Democracies and countries with free speech have always risen up with with unstoppable strength to resist powers claiming their right to control them from outside, as China is doing.

France insulted King Henry V of England, according to legend with three tennis balls instead of promised tribute. Henry invaded and conquered. At that time, the French were spoiled and foolish; their military was no match for England because it was not disciplined.

Scotland revolted against King Edward I and won independence. At that time, the Scottish were selfless and willing to burn their own corn fields and even die; Scotland fought from desperation to not be oppressed while England's disposition of entitlement was no match.

China claims that Hong Kongers are spoiled like the French were under Henry V. Hong Kongers claim they are desperate to escape oppression like the Scottish under Robert the Bruce. Who is right? The next few years will answer that question. But, it could go either way. Nothing is decided.

At this time, however, China is doing certain things, then Hong Kong is responding a certain way while other countries in the world respond in their ways. China believes everyone else is wrong.

Encore of Revival: America, July 27

It takes two to fight. There are two Americas and half of each are choosing to fight.

As early as 2015, more than a few Obama supporters claimed that Trump spoke as did Hitler. He did not, neither in 2015 nor through 2019. But now, Trump does speak so—with the gentle, understanding, compassionate appeal to sense and patience before the bold and courageous grab. That was Hitler and FDR. And, that doesn't prove anything. Perhaps we should say Hitler spoke as Trump, or both as FDR, because this way of speaking is necessary in troubled times, whether a leader be bad or good. Just because Hitler did a good thing to look good does not mean the good thing is not good.

But, if there were any alarm, it is ignored because of the fake alarms set off by loud radicals on the far Left, possibly about half.

Those radicals do not consider consequence. "Solving" a problem the wrong way will only make the problem worse, then deter others from attempting to solve that problem in the future. They don't know. Ignoring laws to get a kind of so-called lawless "justice" will only breed more injustices. They don't notice. Voting ourselves money from the taxpayer treasury bankrupts government, and government bankruptcy always leads to tyranny. They forget. Congressman Louie Gohmert cites history and notes that banning all overt racist monuments and institutions would mean banning the Democratic Party itself. They were never told. A false alarm will cause people to ignore real alarms. They never cared. If there ever were a time for alarm, it is now every bit as much as abuse has drowned out the alarms.

Qualified immunity of the police has been abused and must be reformed—it will be, there is no question of whether, only how. Either it will be abandoned, reformed, or riots will excuse martial law. But, police will not enjoy the protections they abused—and so-called "good" police will not enjoy the protections they allowed other police to abuse. Even the good cops let the corruption linger and fester. Change in police is inevitable, one way or another. The preferred solution to our police problem is the State-trained militia, but that requires people to think on their own.

Still, many defend police qualified immunity. If federal, state, and county governments were to increase accountability for police to qualify for immunity, there would be fewer riots and most police wouldn't want to quit their jobs. But, if there is no qualified immunity reform through the legislative process, we will go down the road of riots and martial law.

As bad as martial law is, and as much as Trump made the final decision, no one supported martial law as much as those who justified it by creating the need—lawless, policeless idealists on the Left, possibly about half. As much as dissent against police threatens the peace, no one supported anti-police movements as much as good police who didn't rise up to confront corruption among their coworkers. Each side of America's divide creates excuses for the other. It seems like conspiracy, but we can't be sure yet.

We will know whether there is a Trump conspiracy by whether Trump loses the general election. If he does, he can dispute it, thus enraging the lawless on the far Left to rationalize even more martial law. A simple, straight election victory would not be so inflammatory and would indicate Trump has no takeover conspiracy. Having kept campaign promises and being the incumbent, Trump must win; it is historical gravity. If he lost, it would have been on purpose.

No one helped Trump get elected as much as Obama. No one helped Obama get elected much as Bush Jr.—and Bush Jr., Clinton—and Clinton, Bush Sr. On it goes as America divides and fights with itself. Both sides are responsible, fars on Right and Left—those who don't think for themselves, possibly about half each. Some are learning to think, whether Left or Right; they are not the problem, possibly about half each.

Cadence of Conflict: Asia, July 27

Bail on Hong Kong, jump to Taiwan. That's the move from everyone.

Britain doesn't bail on Hong Kong, but creates a path for Hong Kongers to bail on Hong Kong. Britain isn't just walking away. By allowing British Overseas Passport holders to easily enter Britain, British Parliament responds as if 3 million British citizens and their families are suddenly in China— basically treating Hong Kong as if it is truly, fully Chinese. Britain ended its extradition with Hong Kong, making it the same as with China. Britain extended an arms embargo to Hong Kong already in place against China.

This is the part that confuses the Chinese. They want the world to recognize that Hong Kong is China, but when countries treat Hong Kong the same way as they treat China, China objects. Consider the mindset that demands: Everyone treat Hong Kong like China, but you interfere if you treat Hong Kong like China. The Chinese don't understand how the world is responding. They never thought the world would respond this way. They think the world is simply being mean and cruel.

Staying consistent is not a part of the Chinese Communist worldview. Consulates do passport services and diplomatic visits, not much beyond that. That's why countries allow them. America says China went way beyond that, claiming evidence of the consulate running a spy ring. Truth or lie, the Chinese thought they could do anything inside their consulate as if they were in Beijing, otherwise they wouldn't need to burn documents before leaving. They don't see America following consistent rules by demanding the consulate close; they only see America as starting a fight.

Western nations at least pretend to operate with universal standards and kept promises. They are far from perfect, but at least they pretend to and their voters expect them to. China doesn't even pretend to operate with universal standards and kept promises. Chinese Communists simply do whatever they decide for each, individual situation, then justify it as either "their right to do what they want" or as "an internal matter" or as "what is best". If China makes a promise, then decides to break it without any notice, then the people they promised object, China calls that objection "interference". Following precedent or promises has no place in Chinese understanding of lawfulness.

Now, ask yourself about a government that insists that it is fair to change the rules throughout the game and without notice. What will mid-level leaders within that government do themselves and expect from their leaders above them and from their subordinates below them? Will their military be able to function with a culture where it is right to change rules at any time? Will ship captains prefer battles for the glory over winning the war? Will the West think such a military is a formidable threat or that such a military is inconsistent and easily defeated?

Taiwan certainly sees the Chinese military as a threat, but the Taiwanese apparently believe China's military can be affronted. Taiwan boosts its own military budget while the US only increases ties. Banks are also looking to Taiwan as the Asian alternative to Hong Kong, which banks are losing interest in since it now appears to be truly, fully Chinese. With so many people running to Taiwan—and taking their money with them—Taiwan won't lack the budget for defense.

So, ask yourself, with the shift moving to Taiwan, what will the rule-changing Chinese do? And, will China's rule-changing embolden the West to think that China's military won't be very organized?

Encore of Revival: America, August 3

The montages and excerpts won't sway a single vote. Congressman Jordan's six minute video mainly shows footage of just a few groups mobbing police with limited looting. This doesn't contradict the narrative on the Left that activists don't primarily loot, but strongly oppose police in particular. Both Right and Left voters think the video justifies their own position. Not one opinion changed.

People are generally fed up with police having an elitist attitude. Trump supporters don't think Trump needs to act for police to get what they beg for, the mobs on the Left are doing a good enough job. There won't be any changed votes over police and protests.

Experts and analysts are starting to predict a possible Trump victory because Trump identifies with the main backbone of swing States. In other words, some people think the energizing incumbent who kept campaign promises might win against a boring opponent. The technical polling research term for that is, "Dah!"

The interesting factor in all this analysis is that Trump supporters don't seem swayed at all by the media. Rich Thau finds that his Obama-Trump focus groups mainly watch local news. And, that explains everything.

The media can't take away what the media did not give. Sentiment for Trump never came from any single speech or opinion. It came from results. People were tired of jobs moving overseas while the so-called spirit of free trade served as little more than an excuse to fatten China into the otherwise unnecessary threat we have today. Now, people are glad jobs are back and someone is actually telling China to behave. People were tired of a Washington culture that talks nice and polite while steamrolling the obvious will of the electorate. People hated bad results before and liked the good results in the last three and a half years. It was the results, not opinion-slanted news from any side, that shaped pro-Trump opinion.

The concept that reporting doesn't decide public opinion is a concept that the reporting establishment can't grasp. All the polls that falsely predict every Republican incumbent's magical defeat can't change people who don't even watch, no matter how much those polls think they can.

Cadence of Conflict: Asia, August 3

If ever there were a time when two nations didn't want to get along, it is now. If ever there were a time when a growing group of nations decided that a single other nation never wanted to get along, it is now.

China's security law affecting Hong Kong, defining what is a crime in every sovereign, non-China territory of the world—in a word "pretentious". No nation's government should ever allow a foreign government to define what is a crime within its own borders, especially a single government acting unilaterally and without counsel.

Human Rights involve laws that China directly agreed to in joining the United Nations. Human Rights sanctions over forced sterilization among Uighurs in Xinjiang in no way compare to Beijing dictating it is a crime for someone in New Zealand to voice support for free elections in Hong Kong. The Confucian-Communist Chinese don't see the difference. They view sterilizing Uighurs as fair and international sanctions for doing so as unfair. It's not a lie or polite statement—they really see things that way.

So, banning TikTok won't give the Chinese any second thoughts about their aspirations and actions. Taiwan's first democratically elected president passed away this week at 97 and the US lauded his achievement. China won't see any need to change so as to cooperate with our democratic world today; they will only see it as an insult to China's entitlement to greatness.

The Taiwanese chip maker TSMC provides 20% of the worlds microchips at quality of which China cannot produce any. If China invaded Taiwan and TSMC had to cease operations, China would suppose that the ability to make these chips would instantly transfer to China, where China could pick up the slack, so there would be no threat to the global tech industry.

Now, the US introduces a bill with bipartisan support for military action already approved for the US to defend Taiwan against China specifically. It's not hard to know how China will respond. With every step, China has the same response: China's right; the rest of the world is wrong. It's not hard to know how the rest of the world interprets that kind of response.

Encore of Revival: America, August 10

The pneumoniavirus is scheduled to finish by the end of October—at least that's what it would seem like from international news. India, Mexico, Great Britain, even the US—October's end and the pneumoniavirus's end coincide with a great number of predictions, plans, lockdown spans, and, don't forget, America's election season.

Did Trump really lose a donor? Reports that he did come only from people commenting on his side of a single phone call. Remember, no one makes the amount of money under discussion by being offended. We must choose to either be offended or be rich; this donor's choice was obvious.

There's no way in money's green Earth a man who has given so much and made so much more would change his strategy of our political future and security based on a misunderstanding in a single phone call. But, the voters such a rouse is meant to target haven't learned that. The political establishment class seeks to keep poor people poor by playing on common misconceptions about the wealthy, rather than trying to educate the masses on the easy and simple principles of success. If you want to win, never let yourself get offended. No one is ever as offended as the bull about to die in the ring of a bullfight.

Beirut—there's too much suspicion. The proximity of the grain storehouses, the fact that half of the shock wave went safely out to sea, why an undelivered shipment wasn't removed to save the expense of wasted warehousing on prime real estate, and an aloof political class to easily blame—conspiracy theories can't not fly. It's not about evidence of conspiracy, but rather circumstances that sing in unison. This tragedy will provide valuable telemetry to indifferent researchers in the context of escalating global tension. What will cities look like when bombs go off? Thanks to this "accident" in Beirut, we now know. Motives and alibis are everywhere.

The yeah-boo is that Lebanese are accustomed to living in a war-ravaged country. They will shine through this smelly tragedy better than most in the West would—with sorrow, perseverance, and well-earned grudges. The West will watch, help, and hopefully learn. Maybe some of us will learn to shine from the Lebanese people.

Cadence of Conflict: Asia, August 10

China received two-and-a-half slaps in the face this week: financial sanctions against a few Chinese and Hong Kong leaders, who don't have money in the US anyway, and the first formal diplomatic visit from America to Taiwan in over 40 years. To add "insultlett" to insults, the purported reason for the US visit was to discuss health and disease cooperation in the face of the Wuhan-famed pneumoniavirus, with Taiwan being the safest place in the world from the disease.

All of these actions from the US are perfectly understandable.

Countries should visit each other. The US is wrong for not having visited Taiwan over the last two score, just as North and South Korea are wrong for their tensions. The world needs people to talk to each other, whether in government, religion, or otherwise. At least Taiwan and the US seem to be getting along much better than Democrat and Republican voters in America.

Sanctions over Hong Kong's turn of events are also understandable. Beijing doesn't have jurisprudence over the world, but certain people in Beijing seem to think so and aren't afraid to put their opinions in ink and law. No, Americans shouldn't do business with such folk; no one should, no matter what country they're from.

As understandable as US actions are, they are nonetheless provocative. We can't expect Beijing to be happy. America found the perfect storm, and bet the bank that people in the Pentagon know what's going on. But, something seems different in this week's volley of cross-Pacific insults: Beijing didn't pop a hernia like it usually does.

Could the Chinese Communists be learning to not feed taunts from the US? Or, more likely, has Beijing read the clear message of actions and decided to quietly plan retaliatory "messages" of action in ways other than rhetoric? The next few months will tell us.

Encore of Revival: America, August 17

The ability to attain and maintain peace is special, especially these days. It's what government should do, but doesn't always know how. The police in Kalamazoo, Michigan did the right thing by being close enough to act if needed, but not being the "main event". The role of the police is to preserve the peace, not to prevent the consequences of a radical group choosing to provoke another radical group. Conflict only lasted 10 minutes, then quickly calmed down. Less could be said for other parts of the nation.

Our president's brother passed away at 71, God rest his soul. As the family grieves, business in the nation continues.

Israel now has formal ties with the UAE, which could mean direct flights between Dubai and Jerusalem. The Palestinians aren't happy; the world isn't surprised. This affects the Unites States on the international stage as well as the election. Foreign relations help at the ballot box.

Biden has all but formally announced the VP nominee. It won't matter because he doesn't stand a chance of winning. Headlines about the Democratic ticket doomed to fail do little more than distract Democratic voters who don't know they have been duped by the media into a false hope based on false fears and slanted polls. But, those lies sure do sell newspapers!

Trouble is on the rise. It comes in spurts, but it is growing. People are moving out of Californian cities. Protests continue in Portland and Seattle. The trouble is complex, much of it is deserved, and much of it is necessary for our nation to confront the issues that keep us from healing from our past. The only way out is through. To do that, we'll need to listen to each other.

Cadence of Conflict: Asia, August 17

All of us enjoy the results of the paths we choose, paths which no one can choose for us. Americans believe this so strongly, it often leads to unhealthy apathy toward others in distress. When America finally decides to help others, it is often from a kind of "Messiah" complex, viz Vietnam, Iraq, and Afghanistan. From this American worldview, including the good and the bad, America would have no motive to "keep China from rising". We just don't think about others that much, you see.

Nonetheless, China has frequently claimed its destiny and right to rise to greatness, using this claim as an excuse to threaten, attack, and oppress others, all the while adding another claim that resistance to forced Chinese subjugation is an attempt to "keep China from rising". But again, free-minded people, whether self-absorbed or genuine, have no motive to keep others from rising.

Why do voices from China's government suppose the intended motives of a free-thinking people, which the Chinese Confucian Communists cannot themselves identify with? Is this a random misunderstanding? To suspect ill motives of others toward oneself while at the same time seeking unchecked authority over others is more reminiscent of the *paranoid narcissist**. Adding to that China's legislated policy for Hong Kong, against its UN-registered treaty of 1984, and for Taiwan, of which it still remains unable to assert jurisprudence, we now have signs of Obsessive-Compulsive Disorder. OCD was never about being clean and organized, but rather using excess rules of organizing as a means to control others. Added up, China demonstrates personality disorders from all three clusters.

That is an explosive mix, so to speak.

But, while insanity is a threat to others it is always a greater threat to itself. In addition to narcissism, an over-inflated view of self falls within purview of the Biblical proverb, "Pride goeth before destruction, and a haughty spirit before a fall." We in the West should not fear Chinese aggression, rather the fallout of narcissistic rage as China painfully learns that it cannot be a worldwide dominator. That lesson may cost a tuition of lives in the millions.

Yes, we are going down this path. August 15, this past weekend, marked the 75th Anniversary of Japan's surrender to the United States and serves as a reminder of Western resolve to stop the map from changing. Almost four years prior, Japan had provoked the West against the wise advice of China; today, those roles seem reversed. We have no reason to fear, but we must be honest with ourselves enough to be ready for what has been brewing a long time.

*https://www.psychologytoday.com/us/blog/
spycatcher/201805/living-the-paranoid-narcissist

Encore of Revival: America, August 24

The US has has taken a hardline on NATO. Of course, NATO members love to criticize the nation that pays the bills that their economic policies can't afford—or perhaps that their economic priorities refuse.

Germany wants an American debt-funded military and complains like a cat when something is taken away. Everyone wants to negotiate with an Iranian government that actually issued an arrest warrant for the American president. It's not that those nations believe negotiating is an answer; they don't know what the answer is. For them, negotiation is nothing more than their ongoing career habit that guided them through fundraisers and elections.

Europe is largely Liberal anymore. It's like a nest of baby birds whose economic theory is that mamma and pappa bird need to give them more worms—and this is the way to keep the economy going. None of these baby birds demonstrate awareness that worms don't just appear; the adult birds must go find them! The solution is for baby birds to grow up and learn to hunt for worms of their own. But, tell that to European Liberal leaders these days and you'll get a response of aloof entitlement and condescension.

There are ways in which things must be done so that cash flows. Money doesn't move merely because the government told it to. People are driven to invent and pursue dreams and healthy ambitions. Keep them from killing each other, stay out of their way, and then they will gladly generate profit on which they gladly pay enormous taxes.

Ambition is unimaginable to a baby bird who thinks it will never be able to fly simply because it never has. Lucky for us, many Americans are growing up. But, Europe might not grow up in time.

Cadence of Conflict: Asia, August 24

These days, Taiwan is the perfect poster boy in China bashing. Yes, China needs to be confronted. No, China can't own the world. Yes, China wants to own the world. Yes, China responds to anything and everything like a friendless student carrying a Grandiosity complex. But, that doesn't mean mindless China bashing will help.

We are engaged in mindless China bashing.

Learn from Germany. WWII developed because the free world punished and insulted Germany after WWI. We need healing, gentle leadership, and grace. Trouble maker countries must be coached and guided, not merely insulted and smeared. Whatever conflict we see with China on the horizon, it will only grow back with a vengeance if we fail to handle it correctly now.

In the China bashing narrative, Taiwan is the perfect innocent—the victim everyone pities. Poor little Taiwan struggles to stay afloat with the tsunami of Chinese conflict. But, as part of that narrative, don't deify the poster boy.

Taiwan has many of its own problems that go unreported. It's people are friendly in many ways, but also oblivious. Success with the pneumoniavirus developed a Royalty complex, where Taiwan has a higher regard for itself without understanding the foreign nations that struggle with relations, investment, and trade in these times. There is a growing reputation Taiwan's government continues to set for itself and Taiwan will need to face that sooner or later.

Taiwan's troubles are not uninvited. But, when we over-simplify global conflicts, brainwashed thinking wants pure villains attacking pure victims. There is no such thing. And, a peaceful future requires us to stop living a news narrative of fantasy.

Encore of Revival: America, August 31

Indefensible. That's the word for the actions of police who continue the same arrogant conduct, even after all that has happened. It's also the word for the Biden campaign.

A virtual convention that looks like a press conference can't compete with a party convention on the White House lawn. Biden's appeals are too much akin to Carter's at the close of his defeated debate with Reagan. If I didn't know better, I'd say the Democrats want to lose. It's more likely that they don't know when they are losing because they don't know how to adapt. That goes for arrogant police as well as losing Democrat campaigns.

Take careful note of the dissent, complaints, doom-mongering, accusations, and verbal vomit coming against the leaders steering us through these times. This barrage of doubt befits the same ilk any victor faces in the hours and minutes before breakthrough and victory. Remember it well. After Trump wins and does more of what they said could not be done, the same accusers will deny that they ever claimed the inevitable was impossible.

Cadence of Conflict: Asia, August 31

There was always a stark difference between America's southern wall and the Berlin Wall. America's wall was built to keep people out—whether they were desperate to come in or hungry to invade. The Berlin Wall was meant to keep people in—people desperate to escape from the oppression, fragmentation, and poverty that flow from communism every time it's tried.

China's Great Wall is akin to America's southern wall. It was a defense against invaders, meant to keep the Chinese people safe. But today, we see a different force in effect. Chinese patrols in the waters outside Hong Kong remind us of the Berlin Wall, meant to keep in people who desperately want to escape a regime they did not choose.

Before, it was said that America has a new Cold War with China. Now, we know for sure. China has implemented new policy that strives to contain a free-thinking people who fueled one of the most amazing economies China has ever destroyed, let alone claimed credit for.

Others are not standing by. Taiwan is arming up and bunkering down. America, all to glad to help, thumps its chest loudly and often. Australia and Japan promise to act independently, which, though seen as diplomatic distancing from the US, won't make China happy to hear any form of the word "independent".

Dissenting voices against countries that like the word "independent" say China is a benevolence, yet feel the need to add that China must be accepted—forgetting that anyone who needs persuasive words in order to be accepted is not evidently benevolent. So, which is it? Is China benevolent or do we need to be told to accept China because we would not otherwise? Both can't be true, only one. And, the world is making up its mind which.

Encore of Revival: America, September 7

This week, we remember events 19 years ago, while everyone else was running out of collapsing buildings, police and firefighters were running in, never to return. They were exemplary. America needs exemplary again.

Less than two months before America's election, rouse after rouse makes headlines. Trump had a medical emergency at Walter Reed, until he didn't, reported by the same press that followed in his motorcade and knew better. Trump is ending Social Security, except that he's not. Trump is destroying democracy—by doing all the things everyone already knows he's doing—things which Democrat voters always hate and Republican voters always cheer. It might be less frivolous to say that Republicans are destroying democracy, but that wouldn't fit the narrative of having so many "October surprises" in early September.

As for the rouse about fallen soldiers being "losers", Trump gave further credence to an old Pacific Daily Times Editorial theory, that John Kelly was the mole all along. Look back to articles in 2018 on September 10, November 19, and December 10. Pacific Daily Times, we've got your tomorrows.

Remember, when Trump announced in 2015, he was already elected in 2016 and already re-elected in 2020.

Mail-in voting would be a great idea if it didn't have so many opportunities for fraud. Anytime the Left tries to fix something, they do such a terrible job that Republican voters throw a fuss and do it how Republicans could have done, but chose not to do, it in the first place. This time is no exception.

Mail-in voting will wreak of fraud for one reason: The Left didn't make it fraud-proof when they made it. Republican voters see the danger and will use all their powers to prevent election fraud, catching the frauds in the process. It's not a good year to be dishonest.

Cadence of Conflict: Asia, September 7

As Philippa Georgiou said to Leland in the season 2 finale of Start Trek: Discovery, "We were just talking about you. Everybody hates you. Congratulations." It goes without mention which country that statement is most relevant for, today.

The Czech mayor of Prague rebuked China publicly and officially, using profanities. France and Germany did as much, in their less-these-days European forms of "diplomacy". Israel gave the green light on travel to Taiwan, not China—making an even stronger distinction difficult for Beijing to erase. Turkey and Pakistan seek closer trade with Taiwan, not China. Real estate in Hong Kong is crumbling in reaction to a certain law that wasn't made in Hong Kong, but was made in Mainland China.

A Chinese jet reportedly crashed in Guangxi, according to a viral video. Some speculated that the jet was struck by what some think could have been an anti-aircraft defense missile from Taiwan. There was no evidence to this. Taiwan denies this. And, China won't even confirm that a jet crashed. Why?

Could it have been malfunction? Could it have been a US submarine—or a flying saucer—sending a message to Beijing that Chinese reverse-engineered jets are no match against the jets of the West they reverse-engineered? Either way, China has yet another reason to back off, but don't expect it.

Taiwan redesigned its passport to make its proper title "Republic of China" look much smaller, minimizing the word "China" while celebrating the word "Taiwan". This runs contrary to a trend of companies taking strange strides to reflect affiliation with China. Consider *LinkedIn changing the display of "Hong Kong" to "Hong Kong SAR"**, effective October 12, even though it seems strange English wording on a social media site. With airlines and companies like LinkedIn towing the line for Beijing Mandarin-speakers' preference of how the English world should talk, Taiwan making the word "China" smaller on new passports could be considered provocative. It could even be a threat to China's national security—something that proves very easily threatened.

Then, there's India.

The China-India border is starting to look like a siege; the castle wall being the Himalayas. Tanks on each side are in shooting range of the other. Talks are scheduled. And, India said it hoped diplomacy was the best answer while at the same time banning another Chinese social app.

It seems these days that diplomacy is just another hoop to jump through—as necessary as it is useless—on our way to war with a country whose leaders think alienation is the best way to make friends. Short of a miracle, diplomatic or otherwise, war with China seems inevitable.

*https://jessesteele.pdt.news/infocus/linkedin-chooses-hong-kong-sar-for-user-experience/

Encore of Revival: America, September 14

Get ready for more. All history points to Trump's re-election, including the usual Leftist press who predict the defeat of every Republican incumbent who wins anyway.

Half of the American voters' minds are already made up.

Trump supporters don't want to surrender to the utter despotism demanded by the rising kamikaze movement from the uttermost Left. In the past, whenever voters finally saw evidence a Republican candidate was only 99% perfect or less, they voted Democrat. Not anymore!

Anti-Trumpists from the rising kamikaze movement from the uttermost Left have their minds half made up. They won't accept Trump no matter the evidence, no matter the results, no matter the jobs brought back from China, no matter the Chinese invasion repelled by Trump's administration. But, they haven't made up their minds that their boring "Hidin' Biden" candidate won't win by holding conventions over Skype or the like. They don't know when they are losing, possibly because they lack sense of "self". After Trump wins in November, expect the uttermost Left to demonstrate something akin to "narcissistic rage".

Things aren't cooling off anytime soon.

While the uttermost Left destroys themselves in order to destroy everything—or perhaps the other other way around—those not from the uttermost Left finally see the insanity for what it is. Many in the center-Left have concerns about a rising police state. Republicans have let down their guards because they happen to be getting things their way this time around. Republicans might be here to save the day, but they won't save tomorrow. A new political movement must rise to save our future. With people waking up to what the utter Left demands, now we only need to wake up to what the utter Right has ignored. Then we'll be through.

Cadence of Conflict: Asia, September 14

It was only a matter of time. The stories are breaking about Taiwan's inhospitality toward foreigners.

Taiwan has the lowest birthrate in the world. They need people; they need talent; they need support. By denying dual-citizenship to foreigners who would have become dual citizens under similar circumstances in almost any other country, Taiwan is not filled with dual-nationals from around the world.

Czech might send politicians to visit Taiwan, but since there aren't many Czech-Taiwanese dual citizens in Taiwan for Czech to protect, don't expect military support. If Taiwan had immigration policies comparable to the other nations they want help from, they would have many citizens from those countries; but they don't. If the Chinese bombed Taiwan, they would hurt citizens from around the world. China might think twice. But instead, any Westerners in Taiwan are simply expats who have no reason to stay, and it's all thanks to Taiwan government bigotry inherited from an ancient culture made in ancient China.

Taiwan had mistreated and given the red tape runaround toward ESL teachers, European students on scholarship, and who knows what kind of superstitious "cursed black skin" comments have been told to people from Africa. American-born Taiwanese are native English speakers, but denied ESL jobs with the claim "only a White face can teach English". Leave it to Taiwanese business owners to think Chinese-speakers know how to teach English best.

Now, Hong Kong needed help from Taiwan and saw the same bigotry Taiwan refused to address for decades. And in case anyone wondered, that's why Taiwan is on the brink of war with China. The Taiwanese government hasn't built the foundations of justice in society that make an economy resilient to war.

Pacific Daily Times has stories spanning back over a decade. Public appeals have been made and ignored. Recent information says that Taiwan has zero progress in changing its bigotous immigrant policies. But, the Times chooses not to elaborate on the recent resurgence of this decades-old problem for one reason: America's election.

Such a problem so old should not be overshadowed by routine election cycles. It must not be said that a problem spanning back thousands of years should come up—of all times—two months before the 2020 American presidential election. Taiwan's ancient-Chinese bigotry must not be reduced to an October surprise.

Taiwan is worth saving, as Jesus said of everyone. The Taiwanese people are amazingly friendly toward foreigners—as long as the Taiwanese are either younger or international, or if the foreigner is White and rich and neither student nor ESL teacher. Taiwan has the potential to change and improve, just as America was among the first nations to ban the human sin of slavery, starting with its own. But, Taiwan must make the choice for Taiwan.

Will there be war in Taiwan? One cannot understand our times while refusing to account for the God who holds all time in His hands. From Deuteronomy, He commands fairness for the widow, the orphan, and the foreigner. And, that God can't be called on to protect Taiwan until Taiwan has protected those who called.

Whether there will be armed conflict between Taiwan and China will depend on the Taiwanese democracy. Their government must make sweeping and instant changes to bring current what good things should have long happened to their foreigners from the nations they call on for help. If such sweeping justice is not given to foreigners in Taiwan by November 4 Taipei time, then Taiwan's neglected past will be both neglected and newsworthy. In that event, Pacific Daily Times will dive into Taiwan's ugly past to explain why Taiwan was weak enough that war from China was feasible in the first place. Let's hope it doesn't come to that.

So, will there be open war between Taiwan and
China? That's something not even God can decide,
only Taiwan.

Encore of Revival: America, September 21

Justice Ginsburg is dead at 87, God rest her soul. Her life's work is well documented in the litany of eulogies from this past weekend. This article will not attempt to add to them.

Whenever a seat opens on the Supreme Court, the nation enters the same debate with the same platitudes. Depending on who is and is not in control of the White House and the Senate, different people argue different platitudes. In 1992, then Senator Joe Biden argued what is today called the "Biden Rule", that supreme justices should not be appointed during an election season. Republicans didn't agree. Then President George HW Bush appointed a justice anyway, along with many other federal judges. The Democrat-controlled Senate, and the Judiciary Committee chaired by Biden, refused to even hold hearings on HW Bush appointees. But, their refusal was not limited to the 1992 election year; Biden applied his "Biden Rule" in 1991.

Then, in 2016, Biden opposed Republicans following the "Biden Rule". He wanted Obama to appoint a justice for the Republican Senate to approve. Suddenly, Republicans agreed with the "Biden Rule" and Biden did not.

Now, a Republican president can appoint a justice for a Republican Senate to approve; but some Republican Senators think they should follow Biden's rule. Democrats would never follow Biden's rule if they had the White House and the Senate; we only expect this from Republicans.

Let's cut with the platitudes and pretentious precedents already. Politicians choose judges because they can. Just how the court always rules in favor of the court—on every case, making whichever ruling reasserts the power of the court— the Senate always votes in favor of the Senate and the White House always acts in favor of the White House.

As with HW Bush and Obama, President Trump will appoint a new justice. The Senate will drag its feet, pretend to serve the will of the people, and play other games to remind Washington that the Senate has power to approve court nominees.

While branches of government put their power on exhibition, the Far Left is resorting to chaos and lawlessness as its display of power. That will only embolden the Right to vote in more Republicans, who will be all too glad to give Trump and his successors the very power he hasn't used, which the Left nonetheless fears he will. Having been nominated for the Nobel Peace Prize as the first president in 39 years not to involve America in the very new wars the Left criticizes the Right for, their case against Trump no longer holds water.

If, by some miracle, Republicans lose the election,
they will approve Trump's nominee anyway. They'll
have to. Notwithstanding that nominee vetting
often takes 70 days, the Senate will likely find an
excuse to wait until after the election. It's not so
much about politics and election strategy as it is
about asserting power by delaying power to expand
power. Expect a Republican-appointed justice by
December, no matter what political smoke blows in
the meanwhile. God rest her soul, Ginsburg is
dead; so is Roe v Wade.

Cadence of Conflict: Asia, September 21

Taiwan has become the center of China's conflict with the world. One economy at a time, one government at a time, China has managed to insult the world. The Chinese have done such a good job of losing friends and alienating voters of foreign countries, not even Russia can afford the political cost of siding with China, not even to manipulate China behind a mask of feigned friendship. Don't expect Moscow to take center-stage at China's aid quite yet.

While the world hates China more and more every day, that hatred finds a way to express itself in love for Taiwan. Taiwan is now the grand alternative! Taiwan is the adorable poster puppy everyone should have sided with from the beginning. Taiwan needs military help, but most of all sympathy, compassion, and understanding, perhaps even grandstanding. Nothing sends the message that a nation is fed up with China like siding with adorable, cuddly Taiwan, especially on the most trivial things like medical masks or forcing Taiwan to call its team "Chinese [what the heck] Taipei" at the Olympics. Trivial things, after all, are what China loves to claim as some of the greatest threats to Communist-controlled national security.

It's almost to the level of being an election tactic in Western democracies. Do or say something that couldn't even hurt a fly, then China squeaks and bellows and throws such a fuss, voters love whichever politician China hates. Nothing is as adorable and benign as kindness toward Taiwan. So, that's the story of how Taiwan became the world's new favorite.

Encore of Revival: America, September 28

It took one week, but we finally have a SCOTUS nominee—the long time nominee apparent, Amy Coney Barrett. The Senate will begin confirmation hearings after waiting another two weeks. Then, hope to vote another two weeks after that on October 26. That will leave the perfect amount of time for Republican voters to get nervous, Democratic voters to worry themselves out, and a few days for all voters to learn that Senate Republicans did what Republican voters wanted. Yes, the Senate dragged its feet and showed its power by delaying power. SCOTUS will be full with 5-3 Conservative justices just before the election, rather than just after. If the Senate was in a hurry, McConnell would crawl over broken glass to begin hearings immediately.

This opens up a myriad of suspicions. If the election is challenged, the court will have six Republican-appointed "original intent" -minded justices, including the notorious swing vote, Chief Justice John Roberts. All six justices vote according to process and intent, usually with Republicans, but not always.

The three remaining Liberal judges, all of them appointed by Democratic presidents, always vote against Republicans and in favor of Democratic-

Liberal ideals, regardless of "original intent". They believe this is honest and ethical. But, they won't be deciding any election disputes, the six rule-stickler justices will.

A Left-leaning professor this week observed that Trump acts much tougher than he actually is—and that Democratic voters should stop going for his bait. They might not be able to not go for the bait. But, knowing that the election won't change the Supreme Court balance this time around, plus considering how boring Biden is, Democratic voters might not have the energy to show up to vote, not even with the October surprise about Trump's taxes, which won't change anyone's mind anyway.

Cadence of Conflict: Asia, September 28

There are no new developments with China, only old squabbles. China is shouting louder and louder, and Western media publish more in-depth stories outlining the many countries China has squabbles with. China is losing over the TikTok ordeal, as well as companies that helped build artificial islands which were not supposed to be military bases anyway, but somehow became military bases anyway. Sanctions fly from the US, as well as diplomats to Taiwan.

At the UN, Russia said a few words leaning in China's direction, but that's quite a tall order to expect Russia to devote resources helping China win every territorial squabble with India, Taiwan, the US, and Japan. Russia will more likely condemn the West with soft tones, then offer China moral support after its inevitable humiliation.

Humiliation is a funny thing. That seems to be China's perspective all around. China feels humiliated and thinks humiliating others will solve its humiliation problems at home. China wants to own Taiwan because China feels humiliation for various and sundry reasons often created in attempt to escape humiliation. China may even think a Taiwan "D-Day", or "T-Day" would lead to victory—forgetting that Normandy was about free allies reclaiming lost land from expansionists. China has no alliance, China would be the expansionists, and the free people would be defending their homes. Humiliation blinds us and drives us to do crazy things. Russia knows this and plays for any opportunity—not to help China, but to manipulate China through the paradigm of humiliation China just can't let go of.

Encore of Revival: America, October 5

People need to see their leader. It's a national security issue. Is the one in charge alive and well? Rumors about Kim Jong-Un's health often send tremors of doubt through and around North Korea. We don't want the same doubt in America. Doctor's, however, have a narrower and more specific perspective.

Presidents get sick. This is something that happens to almost every president sooner or later. Not if, but when it happens, gossip columns circle questions about transitions of power, mostly to capitalize on curiosity from the country.

President Trump's diagnosis with the pneumoniavirus will lionize him in the minds of the electorate. Now, he is more involved and affected by the virus and is no longer an outsider. He is the victim of China and champion of the people. That's the political script playing out. It can't hurt him in the election, only boost his numbers—because of how he responds.

He learns. He stays strong. He takes precautions. He hates the unpopular masks. He defies doctors' orders—something most Americans love doing. He quarantines himself—something most Americans identify with. He keeps working—because we're all depending on him. Without this response, he would have hurt his own numbers. He chose to respond with "involved strength". Everything is okay if we make it okay, and that's what the president did.

As for the Senate, they found their excuse to step up the suspense and delay of confirming Amy Coney Barrett. Isn't that a politically miraculous coincidence!

Equally coincidental are China and Biden. Neither can say bad things about a man who is sick in the hospital. That'd be like punching a man with glasses. China has to roll back its aggression in the South and East seas or else be seen as an even greater aggressor by the rest of the West.

It's funny how things always seem to work out. None of this was planned, not in the least. It was all a miraculous, convenient coincidence. Nothing more.

Cadence of Conflict: Asia, October 5

The world is entering a realization phase: China doesn't care what the world thinks or how the world responds. Beijing has become that annoying kid at school who has no friends, and his solution is to be more annoying. The sad part is how the West allowed us to get here. Coupon-clipping consumers buying cheap products are just as much to blame as governments who believed giving money to the Confucian Communists who control China wouldn't feed their narcissist outlook.

But, China has been warned. And, we each hold the greater responsibility for our choices and actions.

While China makes its choices, Taiwan deals with its own demons of the past. China is not the only society in the Far East self-chained by Confucianism. Taiwan's Confucian culture empowered them to adopt xenophobic laws, keeping foreigners limited and weak and unable to contribute to the Taiwan economy. Confucianism also indoctrinates students to hate questions in the classroom and at home, while touting parroted answers as "wisdom". That runs contrary to innovation and the inquiring mind needed to invent new technology. As a result, Taiwan is much weaker than it could have been without

Confucianism, making it appetizingly vulnerable to predatorial China. Taiwan now faces a choice of whether to correct its self-imposed, Confucian-born limits of the past.

In some sense, the China-Taiwan conflict is an internal matter, but not purely. China plans to retake Taiwan with Western money and American dollars, after all. The world cannot sit by and watch two self-crippled societies cannibalize each other. The world won't sit by and watch, not any longer. And, that is something the Confucian Communists of China don't understand because, at this point anyway, they are not so capable.

Encore of Revival: America, October 12

The Democrats are desperate. In the vice presidential debate, Kamala Harris promoted a delusional sense of peace with China, describing Obama's policy to empower China to grow strong and aggressive as the means of peace, blaming China's aggression on Trump's policy to disrupt China's decade of aggression. From Harris's perspective, time travel would be necessary because she blames Trump's enforcement of basic respect for China having built military islands and aircraft carriers during the Obama years, which are now used to threaten war against any country not accepting Chinese Communist censorship of free speech. Perhaps she doesn't think China has been bullying its neighbors; or perhaps she knows, but she thinks the American voters don't know yet.

Talking as if we all need to "get along" to solve the problem of a sinking ship seems wise to people who don't know their ship is sinking. Such are Kamala Harris's arguments, along with other Democrats.

Gretchen Whitmer, who was tipped off to a kidnapping plot by the FBI—under the Trump administration—acted indignant, almost as if she believed Trump himself had planned the kidnapping. Regardless of how credible her response wasn't, it is not the response of a party that believes it is winning the numbers for an approaching election. If Whitmer believed Democrats were winning, they would have said something different.

Democratic leaders and candidates are resorting to emotional appeals in their public statements. This is the most convincing indication that Democrats themselves believe they are facing a major loss in November.

Cadence of Conflict: Asia, October 12

China has gone effectively "NR", a tech term for software being "non-responsive". No matter what any nation says or does, China only digs in, tells the same lies no matter how increasingly obvious, and continues aggression as the solution to losing more friends over its aggression.

Why censor Mike Pence's statement on China during the vice presidential debate? As an act of good will, China should replay Pence's statement to correct for the ostensible "no signal please stand by" message during that part of the debate. If anything, letting a foreign vice president make bad statements would help prove that China does not engage in free speech censorship. In all likelihood, the Chinese have been censoring so many people and getting away with it that they thought censoring the American vice president would go unnoticed—it didn't.

Besides, why keep a foreign vice president's words away from the ears of their own people. The Chinese people won't decide how the West will respond to Chinese aggression; the West will decide how the West responds. That's something else the Chinese Communists don't seem to understand.

Four nations held a strangely, vaguely-purposed meeting: Japan, Australia, India, and the United

States. The reason went largely unexplained, though it was obviously about China. Japan said the meeting wasn't about one, single country. Australia said no one tells Australia what to do. The US said China is dangerous. From a Chinese Confucian Communist perspective, the meeting seemed out of order. But, in the minds of Western voters, it is clear that all four countries dislike China without having to be told to. It was an unencrypted message China was sure to not decrypt.

Encore of Revival: America, October 19

TV numbers and ratings tricks are all the Left has left. While one October surprise after another surfaces, they mostly favor Republicans. The Left's work is in ratings. It seems to some that Liberals double and triple-up on media devices to give artificial boost to Biden ratings. And, it doesn't seem out of character for Liberals, but the question is: Why?

The Leftist mind believes that people believe what they believe for a combination of two reasons: 1. because people were told to believe a thing and 2. because other people believe a thing. It's almost as if Liberals see themselves as a permanent majority by voluntary opinion—an opinion they chose to adopt because everyone else is doing it. That also explains why Liberals believe Trump stole the election—they believe they are the assumed and permanent majority, so any opposition must therefore be very small and even more so rare. If TV numbers favor Trump, they must lie to create false TV numbers to accurately reflect the truth—because the truth needs their help—everyone needs their help.

By presenting falsely-inflated ratings in favor of Biden, Far Left voters believe they are making Conservatives feel like "the minority they always were and always will be", which the Far Left thinks of as an insult, even though the Left campaigns on the platform of defending minorities. Think about it, if Conservatives really were the minority the Left thinks they are, wouldn't the party that defends minority rights want to stand up for them?

If Liberals scorn Conservatives for being a supposed minority, what does that say about what Liberals think about all the "minorities" they claim to try to help?

Then again, maybe the Leftist mind isn't thinking at all; it's just failing and doesn't know what to do other than keep pretending.

Cadence of Conflict: Asia, October 19

The new global trend is hit pieces against China; even a Taiwanese rapper is on the bandwagon. China's solution to lack of technology is to take over countries that have enough freedom to create technology, then deprive those countries of their freedom in order to get their technology. It's clear China thinks innovation is a commodity rather than an indication of an already liberated people.

Taiwan doesn't need liberated by China; it already has been liberated from China. While the Chinese think that intimidation has driven the Taiwanese into fear, it hasn't. As Taiwanese carry on with life as usual, the word on the street has nothing to do with fear of invasion; the Taiwanese are simply waiting for the Chinese to ask to get their ass handed to them.

The Philippine government wants to drill for oil in the South Sea. China was supposed to do that in cooperation, an old promise that still hasn't materialized. From Xinjiang, we learn that children of detained Uyghurs are being orphaned, and China is now sending them to Confucian brainwashing school. Perhaps that was China's goal in detaining their parents; it certainly worked out that way.

The US is pursuing charges against Chinese espionage in America. China threatens to detain Americans in retaliation. But, that misses the whole point. If China knows about American spies in China, then China should have already taken action anyway. It makes a country look weak to not stop crime except in retaliation. Does China want to send the message that American spies can spy unchecked in China as long as America's government doesn't prosecute Chinese spies caught in America? The world wonders what China wants. Maybe China wants the world.

But, the world doesn't want China's low-tech industry, repulsive actions, controlling conduct, retaliatory justice, Confucian indoctrination, nor forced language. Nations and peoples of the world will use their ability to invent to overcome China's low-tech weapons and easily-offended, easily-intimidated culture. Of course, the Chinese don't know when they are out-teched, out-matched, out-willed, undesired, and surrounded. They already are, but they don't know. The only ones who know are everyone else.

Encore of Revival: America, October 26

Media and analysts miss the greatest takeaways from the debate. Arguments were based on who did what while already in office: All of the problems Trump solved and Biden didn't, but says he will. And, their positions were radically different: Biden appealed to need for help while Trump appeared in-control at the helm.

The only times incumbents lose reelections are in the wake of gross incompetence (not seen since Carter) or gross broken campaign promises (not seen since HW Bush). If anything, Biden appears to already have broken the promises he is now making. That will not be enough to eject a promise-keeping incumbent.

In our last week before the election, polls have gone on record for predicting Biden as voices in media shifted their tone to a non-answer over who will win. Trump already won 2020 in 2015 when he announced. Many people don't understand that. Many in media believe they decide election outcomes, not voters, so they don't understand it either.

The greatest danger Trump always posed was that he would do too good of a job. He is the leader the Republican Party doesn't deserve. They denounced him. He delivered the promised results they wouldn't. Now, they will have respect they didn't earn, plus a near supermajority in the Senate, control of the house, and overwhelming control of the Supreme Court. Power unchecked corrupts. Trump's awesome work will get him reelected where he will continue more awesome work, but awesomeness can destroy us where it is unearned. And, that shadow is where the RNC stands.

The country will likely destabilize over the coming weeks. Americans will fight from anger on all sides. War with China could be seen as a convenient distraction from domestic dysfunction at a time when the US needs an excuse to put an unchecked Asian bully in its place. But, China doesn't need to be embarrassed; it needs to be discipled. But, the US won't be ready to disciple anyone until the US recovers its lost neighborly conscience. The US will find its conscience again, but it appears that we will only learn through trouble.

Cadence of Conflict: Asia, October 26

The flashpoint of Taiwan has become a pregnant possibility. Reportedly, a US military jet flew across Taiwan, and no one is fully certain over who claimed what and why. Taiwan's government said something after the US government said something about the mission. Then the US government said that they weren't saying what the mission was. So, the Taiwan government said that they weren't saying what the US government wasn't saying about what the US government said about why what happened happened. And, we're not even sure what happened because the identifier tags could have been spoofed.

In the end, China fell for the bait as if on cue. The Chinese State-run Global Times then published a story sometimes written in the first-person stating that the US isn't allowed to fly military operations over Taiwan and that China would send its military planes over Taiwan if the US did. The story went on to speculate that Taiwan didn't have the unction—more or less—to fire the first shot at a Chinese plane in Taiwan sovereign airspace. That proves what China is really thinking about: pushing and pushing, trying to call Taiwan's bluff, wondering who will fire the first shot—because China is hoping someone will fire the first shot.

After all the information China gave away about its intentions—after what seemed like a fluke between Washington and Taipei—don't think for a second that said fluke was not a well-calculated fluke. The bigger takeaway is that China keeps falling for the bait while Washington learns to anticipate China enough to lead the Chinese Communist military right into its own defeat—and China shows the learning curve of a cat chasing a laser dot.

Encore of Revival: America, November 2

In the final week before the election, polls and mainstream news articles made every effort to paint a Trump victory as a bigger surprise than his first. He is an incumbent who kept campaign promises and wasn't a failure in the minds of his own supporters. Historically, his defeat is impossible. Mail-in ballots being favored by one party—the losing party—wouldn't ring of fairness. If the incumbent doesn't win, it's a shoe-in coordinated fraud case between both Democrats and their loud supporters in the news industry.

This election will be contested by the losing party's supporters. The media will be part and parcel to any Democratic Party efforts, largely evidenced by attempts to dampen the story of Hunter Biden's laptop. Glenn Greenwald resigned from the news company he helped found. Twitter censored link sharing for the story. Being Democratic-leaning, such institutions can't present the defense that they are without allegiances in an election dispute.

Mail-in ballots are a great idea, not insecure or unsolicited mail-in ballots as we have seen. But, these mail-in ballots have been used and promoted heavily and only by Democrats. That betrays their purpose. If mail-in ballots are responsible for tipping the election against Trump, any fraud case would also include a smoking gun. In that event, the Supreme Court would play an important role.

The Constitution defines Election Day so that everyone knows when it happens. If voters need to mail-in ballots for any reason, they have no excuse to be late. Collecting mail-in ballots after Election Day can't serve any fair purpose and only stinks of mischief.

Recently appointed Justice Barrett abstained from a ruling that would have decided that Election Day happens on Election Day, and Chief Justice Roberts can always be counted on to vote with Democratic prerogatives when it matters. This happens not because justices are Democratic or Republican, but because the Court always rules in favor of the Court. Via split vote, SCOTUS continued election chaos, thereby reminding the nation of the power it wields.

Still, the Supreme Court now seats 6-3 in favor of Republican-appointees. Barrett abstained, claiming she lacked sufficient time to review an expedited case. She can't be counted on to abstain in a post-election dispute. Republicans are growing in power. And, power corrupts.

The RNC spent extra money on the Michigan Senator race—a state where the Democratic Governor is highly controversial. A general election —combined with a Senate election—is a likely place for voters to lash out against the current controlling party. Something similar happened when Republicans lost the House in 2018. If

Michigan goes Republican again, it would indicate a strong turn for other states, including Pennsylvania.

No matter the election outcome, Republican voters will argue legitimacy and Democrat voters will cry injustice. The nation will soon spiral into chaos as this is the hottest time and the hottest election in American history. We will come out the other side, having dealt with many submerged problems which have finally surfaced.

Cadence of Conflict: Asia, November 2

China, China, China. What is the world to think? As a condition of formalizing relations between the United States and Communist-controlled China, US law mandated weapons sales to Taiwan. Now, China is angry that the US upheld this law. Would they prefer the US to break the agreement and shift formal relations back to Taiwan?

In response to the required weapons sales, China sanctioned Boeing's weapons sector, which China buys nothing from. The sanctions did not cover the sector of Boeing where China buys the planes that its Confucian-Communist-oppressed culture does not know how to build. Now, Beijing argues that military planes must fly through Taiwan-controlled airspace and over the island of Taiwan. And, if Taiwan were to fire upon these planes, it would mean war. Do the Chinese believe that the world believes that?

If two countries have a territory dispute, but are not engaged in an armed conflict, then one side of the dispute sends military equipment and personnel into territory controlled by the other side of the dispute, the rest of the world will see the invader as the perpetrator and villain of any armed contest that ensues. If China doesn't back off, the world will blame China. This is not an opinion or preference; it is a fact of the future based on history, but Confucian-Communists can't see the difference between history, opinion, and propaganda. And, that makes anticipating the future nearly impossible for them. China will be shocked by what was obvious to everyone else. It has always been that way.

China is not only fighting Taiwan nor only India nor only Japan. China is fighting the world. And, China doesn't know China can't win against the world. These are dangerous times. That's the one thing everyone knows.

Encore of Revival: America, November 9

America faces a reckoning. The same quiet giant that awoke at Pearl Harbor and 9/11 now wakes inside the Republican voter base. They rise to stop a problem they created for themselves, still without admitting it. While Republicans will win this round, both sides are right and wrong, and this won't be the final round.

Blacks have not received justice from police killings —which should be at the rate of zero. Republicans could have solved the problem by a simple law: what happened to George Floyd should result in death by public hanging for both police officers in a public square within one week of the incident. Republicans could have rammed through such a law—just like they rammed through the approval of Justice Amy Coney Barrett. Both would have been good; they only did one.

Democratic voters can't win this one—not because they aren't in the White House, but because of the difference in battle cries. Democrats have been protesting for years, then many have been looting and rioting in their name. Republicans are weary. Calling to defund police rather than immediately reform can't solve the problem and was never going to garner respect. Republican voters won't allow a mob to burn the neighborhood to the ground because of murders on the loose. Republicans refused to stop the murders because none of their families were victims, yet. That would have stopped the mob. Democrats won't trust them.

So, Republicans have a calm, cool, apathetic irritation toward the extremists on the Democratic end. Patrick Elkins, also at the Times, calls them "Ravens"*. Democrats cry victim, then pour gas on the flames of the duplex next door.

Indeed, the nation wreaks of mass voter fraud from Democrats. Former and disenfranchised Democratic Illinois governor Rod Blagojevich said election fraud was common among Democrats in cities. That may not indicate Democratic ethics, just that both Democratic ideals and political machines seem attracted to cities, allowing the DNC to get practiced and build up a habit. The media is in on it, sending now-proven wrong polls before the election, now forecasting a Biden victory on an election to be decided in court. Fake news coupled with vote fraud is all part of how political machines work. They thought they'd get away with it on a national level. They were wrong.

Republicans are in the wrong for failing to be Good Samaritans to Blacks. They didn't stop systemic injustice because they don't see it themselves— they can't; but Westerners see systemic injustice in Taiwan. We can only see systemic injustice when it happens to us personally. That has injured and insulted the minorities Democrats promise and fail to help.

However justified, crying victim and marching to burn down the neighborhood cannot prevail against an aloof, collected, apathetic giant who stays laced when roused to wrath. That giant rose against Japan to stop Germany; now it's rising against the Democratic political machine, but that doesn't make it Jesus Christ. He's not back yet, if you haven't read the news.

*https://patrickelkins.pdt.news/2020/10/09/new-political-distinction-rising-introducing-the-ravens/

Cadence of Conflict: Asia, November 9

China and Taiwan are in a military face-off for a singular reason: xenophobia. Taiwan had everything it needed to counter China without help from the US, but it snubbed foreigners and still continues to do so today. Were it not for the US, neither China nor Taiwan would have limped so far along. China's "miracle" economy was made of money from the US. Taiwan's weapons use technology developed primarily by the US.

As much as both China and Taiwan have benefited from the US, these two countries have some of the most strict laws against naturalizing foreigners. That doesn't include a serious lack of protection against intrusion of immigrants' rights. When Americans—or any other Westerner—or any other foreigner for that matter—finds work in Taiwan or China, companies impose extra rules to take away what few legal rights they have as foreign employees; then government does nothing, it just sits there and watches. In Taiwan, this largely happens with employment. In China, it happens with entire companies.

Even if foreign workers can find a way to survive the onslaught of attacks against their rights, the most they could expect in the end is an elevated residence status—if they are rich. If they aren't wealthy, no chance. Without citizenship, foreigners in Taiwan have few rights—they aren't even allowed a phone and landlords can reject them merely on the basis of being a foreigner.

China aside, if Taiwan allowed, then protected a path to citizenship for Westerners working in Taiwan, those naturalized citizens would have had more rights to work and contribute to Taiwan's culture, language, economy, and technology. If that had happened, it very well could be the US seeking to buy weapons from Taiwan, and China might be more inclined to behave.

The same could be said of China, which has made itself so desperately dependent on US money by keeping foreigners within their own borders at an arm's length.

This conflict between Taiwan and China was caused by xenophobia from both sides. By not demanding equal respect toward Americans in their borders, but engaging in trade and weapons sales anyway, the US allowed two kittens to grow into a bobcat and a tiger. And, now the whole world faces a huge cat fight—whenever China decides to take advantage of the election ambiguity in the US and bust a foolish move against Taiwan.

Encore of Revival: America, November 16

Elections are not decided by news desks. They are decided by the electoral college, which meets in mid December. Electors sent there are chosen by the State based on election results certified by each State. If an election is in doubt, the decision goes to State legislatures, pursuant to the *Electoral Count Act (1887)* and a Supreme Court interpretation from *Bush v Gore (2000)*.

Judges don't decide whether election results are certifiable; State legislatures do. The burden is not on the Trump campaign to prove vote fraud to judges. The burden is on the polling stations to prove there was no fraud to State legislatures.

Right now, five key states are in severe doubt concerning polling credibility: Wisconsin, Michigan, Pennsylvania, North Carolina, and Georgia. Republicans control the legislatures of all five. And, Trump just backed McDaniel to continue as RNC chair. Perhaps she will have some sway over those Republican legislatures.

Republicans don't have an option. Gross suspicions of election cheating have caused the Republican base to turn away from Fox News to Newsmax. News networks wouldn't call Georgia or North Carolina, even though it looked long past the time it seemed reasonable. To Republicans, this is a conspiracy to institute nation-wide political machines, which they can't accept. In their minds, if they let Democrats steal this election, there will be no more fair elections, and the only way to escape would be an armed revolution. There is no scenario in which the Republican base allows Trump to lose. If Trump gave in, they would turn against him also.

Democratic voters aren't about to tuck tail and turn. Emboldened by a news industry, that insists on its own ability to declare an election outcome, the DNC base only builds for greater disappointment. They don't have the power to decide disputed elections, but they think they do. They haven't already won, but they think they have. Note cautiously, the media does not hope to sway the election outcome, but to sway a revolt for when Trump inevitably wins—a revolt from, of all people, the gun haters.

In order for Trump to lose, he would have to bow out, then Republican voters would take up arms and the RNC, seen as an obstruction, would be dissolved by its base. When he does win, Democrats voters will riot. In either scenario, we are looking at martial law in the coming weeks and months.

But, the question remains: Why was there such gross election ambiguity specifically in states with Republican-controlled legislatures? It's almost as if the entire election controversy were staged. But,

the reason remains yet to be seen, unless the
answer is: China.

Cadence of Conflict: Asia, November 16

America is one of the most cunning nations, almost as much so as Britain. Chinese are known for signing contracts early, then negotiating after—something the West calls "reneging", which breaks the contract. London always knew China wouldn't be able to keep a promise, let alone a promise to not control and interfere.

But, almost as cunning is the appearance of election-based chaos stirring in America. Republican and Democratic voters have been building mutual hatred for a long time. Fighting within the country is real and believable. It was sparked by ambiguity, the cause of which is easily explained by what appears, for all intents and purposes, as vote fraud. That doesn't take much manipulation of the masses, only a small push to send society tumbling over the ledge of insanity. And, China was sure to believe it.

But, there is a difference between America and China which the Chinese cannot understand: centralized power. Chinese-based governments, including democratic Taiwan, struggle to think outside the box of micromanagement. China doesn't know that the US Navy in the Indo-Pacific region is capable of operating and responding, even if all communication is cut off from Washington. That was the purpose of the "boomer" submarines.

The Chinese people are beaten down. It's a culture-wide mental state akin to groupthink Stockholm syndrome. The Beijing government truly believes the Chinese people will never rebel. So, when they see America in disorder, they will think democracy itself has failed. But, they don't understand that the people of a nation are always stronger than the institutions they create, including government, which only derives its power from the people who allow it to be so powerful. Not only can America's government continue to function with American society in a level of chaos, China's government cannot be stronger than its own beaten-down people.

If China wanted to be strong enough to stand against America, it could have started by living up to the name of its army and actually "liberating" its people from a culture in which everyone is an oppressed-oppressing slave. Yes, America can deal with riots at home and kick China's ass in the Pacific at the same time. China doesn't think so; that's exactly what the Pentagon hopes.

Encore of Revival: America, November 23

Friday, Sidney Powell said she will present legal evidence in court within two weeks. Her claims of evidence and testimony for vote fraud far surpass the never-proven claims of the Russianewsgategate scandal. The catch is in the process; evidence in serious court cases is best presented first in court, not first to the press. While interviews and lists of court rulings surface, we can't know the truth of her claims one way or another, yet. Only two weeks will tell.

In the meanwhile, things look grim for anti-Trumpists. While Trump plays golf and Powell behaves as if her claims are the most legit they can be, Giuliani made a statement that Powell is not officially on the Trump legal team per se. Why play golf and clarify that the loudest voice of defense is not on your team? Trump's actions are not those of the Democrats who lost in 2016 nor Bush who lost in 1992. Whatever he's up to, it looks like he is playing it cool with a royal flush in his hand. Whether Trump and Powell are bluffing remains to be seen, but they haven't folded. And, their actions are not those of a loser; Democrats and mainstream media think they are.

Far more important than Trump winning in court are the developments within the Republican base.

They are irate with the Republican Party's inaction.
Perhaps the RNC hopes to manipulate them into
support for Powell's "big reveal" at the end; they
are irate nonetheless. They are a quiet people, not
always prone to shout for Trump at every moment.
And, they are fierce when roused to wrath. More
than these, they have a strange love for each other.

The Sunflower students who took Taiwan's
Legislature in 2014 had the same mutual love, and
with it came "political electricity". Nothing could
stop them.

Neither the Republican nor Democratic parties can
ignore their respective bases. The DNC is doing the
will of its base, even in what Powell portrays as an
attempt to, more or less, institute a nation-wide
political machine. Democratic voters still support
their party. Neither the DNC nor its base can
accept a Trump victory.

The Republican base cares nothing for the
Republican Party, but they will not accept a Trump
loss either. They differ from the DNC base,
however, in their calmness and strange, mutual
love. Democratic voters will be furious and
dangerous; Republican voters will be deadly. Both
are being conditioned for genocidal thoughts
against the other. Republican voters would win
that brawl. The least destructive solution is that
Powell calmly wins her case in court and the RNC
takes supportive action accordingly, but post-
election months still won't be fun.

Cadence of Conflict: Asia, November 23

"Prematurely shredded"—that's how the "Five Eyes" alliance described the treaty allowing Hong Kong to be ruled by China. Canada, Australia, New Zealand, Britain, and the United States have decided that China broke the deal, referring to the 1984 Sino-British Joint Declaration. The danger is in how much China can't understand what this means.

Accusing Confucian-Communists of breaking a promise is like accusing a pig of rooting in its own feces; it doesn't know, it doesn't understand, it can't do differently, and it only feels insulted. The Chinese don't know what a promise is because they never keep them—ever. They only know what they want and that they want it now. They were never going to keep their end of the deal, and Britain knew that, and China played right along.

Broken treaties are no small matter. In a sense, Western nations see it as a blaring stain on a nation's permanent record. Far worse than financial bankruptcy is moral bankruptcy. The West played its hand well, waiting until China overreached time and again, to a point where the evidence was overwhelming, past the point where the people had come to the same conclusion long ago. Western governments can't operate without the will of their people, which is another thing China doesn't understand.

In its attempt at a hostile takeover of the world, China needed the goodwill of the masses. It's action in Hong Kong over the past year stirred anything but goodwill. Western governments will be in trouble with their taxpayers if they don't take action against China.

So, one more stone falls into the arch of Western action against China. With a declared-broken treaty on record, once the Chinese gets their ass handed to them, permanent surrender of Hong Kong—including the New Territories—will be in the growing list of the West's unconditional terms. And, China made it all possible.

Encore of Revival: America, November 30

Left wing and Right wing voters are worlds apart.

The Left are adamant and energized; the Right are as quiet and introspective as America was after Pearl Harbor. The Left believe they have already won an election that hasn't finished; the Right are determined to prevent certain outcomes at any cost. The Left believe that asserting claims that the election is over makes it so; the Right know that results and actions make a thing so. The Right believe Trump acts like he holds a royal flush and will soon bust "the bold move"; the Left think Trump is already neutralized and acts like he's lost. The Left are not armed and trained; the Right have been for eons. The Left know the Right will be angry, but think themselves more powerful; the Right know how dangerous the Left are in riots, yet quietly understand that they themselves would be the more formidable in conflict.

But, the biggest difference is their understanding of sowing and reaping: The Left do not understand how wealth, tax dollars, strength, peace, victory, and justice are cultivated, but take these for granted; the Right know how these are cultivated and that these will cease without correct action. Biden should not be selecting a cabinet for his evermore doubtful presidency; he should be making his seemingly dubious election look less dubious for when it is challenged in court. But not understanding sowing and reaping, Biden and his Left supporters take his victory for granted just as they do tax revenue; the Right know better and are putting their effort where it will make the difference.

News companies, such as CNN, use descriptive terms like "unfounded conspiracy theories" and "insidious claims" in reporting accusation of election fraud. But, these terms imply verdict and opinion, having no place in reporting of mere facts and claims prior to court rulings. The Right see that; the Left don't see the difference. A cross-industry attempt at pushing an agenda is unabashed. The Right feel backed into a corner, believing if they concede this election, there will be no fair elections in the future and that the cost of civil war to restore elections will only increase with time, so they feel compelled to action now; the Left think the Right are not any threat worth notice.

The Right view claims of fraud as plausible and worth investigating; the Left already think the claims are a hoax because they don't understand how accurate investigation works. While the Right reflectively wait for evidence to be shown in court, they see a Left wing agenda that would sow the seeds of destruction which Left wing voters don't believe will happen. Biden's decisions would give rise to Eastern communism and Middle Eastern terrorism, as happened with Obama; the Right think so and the Left do not because the Left do not understand how global results are created. The Right will rise up with its various powers to successfully stop Biden's decisions—one way or another, preferably peacefully—, but the Left do not believe the Right can succeed because the Left do not understand how conflicts are waged and won.

The Right created their own enemies on the Left by refusing to give justice to problems they would not acknowledge. They have not punished "bad cops" enough to restore faith in law enforcement, yet they demand action to restore faith in elections. The Right are competent, but selective with justice; the Left fail at things when refused help and fail more at things they try on their own because they don't know how things work. Both are being conditioned for genocidal thoughts against the other; one is stronger, the other only thinks it is. While the long term danger is an over reverence for a fake Republican party, which cares nothing for the values of its base, a more immanent dilemma is before us. America cannot deal with its own national transgressions if it is taken over by foreign communists and foreign terrorists who are far more unjust in every way. We are in a conflict of competence—the need for policies that will build rather than destroy, even if selective in its justice; only one group understands that, the other only sees injustice.

One way or another, Biden and Harris will not get their way, but they don't know that—they can't know that. Fortunately, there are those who do.

Cadence of Conflict: Asia, November 30

America has China fooled yet again. It isn't hard to figure out, but still ingenious. Whatever strategist first learned it from a convenient mistake that happened with Taiwan. Taiwan's current president, Tsai Ing-Wen, had previously endorsed Hillary, for 2016—a mistake she didn't repeat in the 2020 election. When Trump was elected, Taiwan's government was heavily concerned about retaliation from the Trump administration. But, Americans don't hold grudges nor do we hold high regard for the opinions of foreign world leaders. Tsai reached out to Trump and they soon developed one of the best relationships heads of state ever shared.

China's president, Xi Jinping, doesn't seem to have learned that lesson, however. While many world leaders congratulated Biden when the news industry decided what the future should be, China waited until the GSA got the green light for transition steps. Then, he congratulated Biden on his victory. Taiwan still has not made any move since the electoral college has not convened and remains neutral and welcoming toward whomever the American president will be in January. China's position shows worry mixed with miscalculation.

When Trump's lawsuits, appeal to state legislatures, and near 80% support from his suspecting base land him a second term, China will be in for a shock. They will fear retaliation just as Taiwan did, no matter how unwarranted. This will drive China to take defensive measures without need and appear as the provocateur of the coming US-China conflict. Having served its purpose, US ambiguity over the election will quickly pass, and China's leadership will begin to socially self destruct. Then hold on; things will be furious as they will be fast.

Encore of Revival: America, December 7

Testimony against the Democratic Party -controlled polling stations is, in a word: damning. Trump makes no noise of concession. In his recent Georgia rally, he even took a pot shot at the Republican governor, of whom Sidney Powell was "clarified" off the team after her own shot across his bow. It does look like the Pacific Daily Times theory* that Trump holds a royal flush wasn't far off the mark. Republicans—voters and elected officials alike—support Trump in not conceding. State legislatures hold hearings on evidence and testimony of election fraud. They wouldn't do that if they had already decided to uphold a Biden victory.

While fraud appears to be at the hands of Democrats, the smoking gun sits in the hands of the news establishment. Fringe and startup news groups don't appear to be in on the scandal. But, Chris Wallace insisting that Biden be called "president-elect" prior to the electoral college shows how far things have gone. Mass media, including news and social media, are censoring public opinion and ramming impossible narratives at a level that goes beyond shameless. Google, Twitter, Facebook, and possibly even Amazon and Microsoft are on a fast track to be regulated as public utilities. It has been long coming, but this disputed election will be the last straw to make it happen.

It doesn't take clairvoyance to see where this election dispute is going. Whomever swing states choose, the loser will appeal to the Supreme Court. After the Supreme Court, Trump will win either through a court ruling or an armed revolt. Republican voters won't have a Biden victory. They are the judge and jury in this. Legislatures and courts can only follow the lead of the people. Right now, legislatures and courts are learning that the Republican base is more fear-worthy than the Democratic base for a two-fold reason.

Evidence of fraud indicates that actual Republican support across the nation isn't merely large; it is vast and intimidating. And, as legislatures hear testimony, outbreaks of applause show that this intimidatingly vast voter base is adamant and energized. Such popular energy scares lawmakers and judges. While they act calm and even-mannered in their hearings, and while they have no intention of going against this overwhelming will of the people, the lawmakers and judges are still shaking in their boots. America's government fears its people once again. That's the way a republic oughta be.

See "Encore" for November 23

Cadence of Conflict: Asia, December 7

A date which will live in infamy, 79 years ago. The Chinese warned the Japanese not to attack America for fear of waking a sleeping giant. Now, the Chinese are speeding against their own advice. The move will likely be against Taiwan as a remote and indirect attack on the US. But, the fight between China and Taiwan could have been avoided. The wise can learn from foreseeable history, even when that history has not yet happened.

Taiwan and China are both run by governments with histories of cruelty, corruption, and incompetence. Taiwan is an emerging and aspiring democracy; China resists democracy. Taiwan is cleaning up its cruelty of the past; China increases cruelty today. Chinese Communist tanks killed thousands of unarmed protestors at Tienanmen Square in 1989; that party remains in power through today. Chiang Kai-shek led an even larger massacre in Taiwan in 1947; his party remained in power throughout Western trade and still exists today, though without total control. Now, these two face war. Would either have the money to bloody the other had the West simply demanded justice and order within their borders proportionate to any agreements of trade?

American Congress continues to push a bipartisan and unanimous agenda for Taiwan. The US wants Taiwan to import meat from livestock fed with ractopamine, something Taiwanese want no part of. The US sells weapons to Taiwan to defend against China—which builds its weapons with money made from exports to the US. Has the US been friend or enemy?

If we look at US and Western policy toward China and Taiwan over the last 70 years, we see pursuit of money, with a blind eye toward massacre of their own citizens, xenophobia toward their foreigners, all trailed by escalation toward war. That has improved, but only in the last 4 years and too little, too late.

From 1947 through 1989, Taiwan should have had limited trade, China none. Had that been Western policy, today both might be much more progressed in technology, just, orderly, wealthy, and most of all peaceful.

Taiwanese continue to grow and mature as a democracy. China continues to pursue control and alienate its neighbors. They each have their lessons to learn. But, not all help is helpful. It might not have come to war if the West had sooner insisted that nations learn a few lessons before bestowing wealth which Taiwan and China could have gained on their own with simple justice and order 70 years ago. Instead, we're nearing the end of a path that started with greed and finishes in war.

Encore of Revival: America, December 14

And so, the crud hits the fan. Elections only work with a consensus of trust. A distrusted election result can't work; the masses won't allow it, even if the inaugural ceremonies continue. Neither Trump nor Biden can persist as president past January except in name only. This is how nations split every few centuries. We live to see historic times.

Eighteen states, including Texas, sued the four swing states for illegally changing election rules mid season. If we count the undisputed votes and Republican legislatures of those four states which heard the evidence, that would be twenty-two states for Trump. Twenty-two Democratic states filed to object. If results favor Republicans, the nation is split right down the middle. Each side is convinced it is in the right—Democrats because they saw it on the news—Republicans because they saw it at government hearings which were specifically not on the news. That's all the reason either side has ever needed to believe anything they believe.

Neither side even tried to persuade the other in a way that could be heard. The news-Democrat side simply asserted a result, marginalizing questions as "atypical", ignoring the fact that eighteen states can't be atypical by definition and cannot become atypical by mere assertion. Conservatives and Republican voters argued "evidence" and "rules" after sewing distrust of rules through a century of refusing justice to Democratic voter needs.

Neither side was ever going to concede. The Supreme Court stayed out of it, arguing "lack of standing". Democratic-run states answered with blanket denial one would expect from China—and it seemed to work on the Supreme Court, though it never works when China does it. With the Senate sending a blistering 83 votes against Trump's veto promise on a military bill, Republican voters feel betrayed. Surely, the gun-owning Republicans are mulling over multiple militarized responses. Democrats would riot before conceding. If Trump ever does concede, it would indicate he has plans to eventually win by means more formidable than a militarized option. Concession from either side would be fake, indicating hidden danger to come.

Those eighteen states may boycott the electoral college, denying the two-thirds quorum; if they don't then their lawsuit was only for show. If the Electoral College names Biden, he can rightly be called the "President-Elect" for the first time, even if in question. And, if he gets that title while in question, America will see Conservative rage—and Liberal riots in response—like never before. Liberals aren't fond of following rules when they lose because the rules are unfair against them all too often. Lawless Liberals are somewhat common; lawless Conservatives are a bigger league altogether. God forbid that Liberals break enough

rules to convince Conservatives to stop following
their own rules. That is a wrath none could
prepare for. There is no peaceful resolution, but at
least Americans all agree on the depth of our long-
neglected problems.

Cadence of Conflict: Asia, December 14

Hit pieces against China are coming out as if from an avalanche. More dangerous, they are coupled with Western plans of military expansion in China's back yard. From Xinjiang teens to disappearing journalists to Australian wine to spies in America to colleges—to a global virus pandemic —Western readers have no rest from bad news of China.

The equation has been there and in play. America's election appears stolen to 75% of Republican voters and 30% of Democrats. Elections require agreement on results in order to function. Lack of agreement on a trustworthy election is unusual as it is staggering. That's a mandate for Trump to take drastic action, deny Biden's inauguration, and take measures to remain in office that can't avoid national inflammation.

As inevitable American conflict in January comes into closer view coupled with such bad press on China, the US strategy in the West Pacific is more and more difficult to deny. China was always the perfect distraction from the mess at home. The problem is that the American populous no longer responds as usual. A national attack may not have the uniting effect it once did—at least not uniting enough to keep any president in office in the face of an election so disputed.

Taiwan continues the role as the "China virus" poster boy. The Taiwanese handle things so well, don't they. Strict rules on breaking quarantine—punishing a foreigner with thousands in fines for walking in the hallway outside his room for eight seconds—but Taiwanese officials forgot to lock the quarantine door because the world is supposed to believe Taiwan is so careful, right?

At some point, it should become obvious that we are playing a game of charades with who is good and bad—or at least on who is how good and how bad. As China's role is to be the common enemy for divided Americans and a divided West to unite against, China's big mistake—over decades and to this day—was to play that role all too gladly. A shoe was made and China chose to fit it.

Encore of Revival: America, December 21

Trump has a realistic path to the presidency. Rules for the electoral college allow for discussion and dispute which could delay finalization of the vote past January 18. If Congress has not approved the electoral college vote by then, the electoral college fails and the election defaults to Congress. Then, the Senate chooses the vice president and the House chooses the president by state delegates—of which there are more Republican. At that point, it would be political suicide for even Romney to vote against Trump. All that has to happen is delay in the Senate—something the Senate is very good at when it wants to be. With 18 states having filed a suit with the Supreme Court, such a delay is quite likely.

Far more interesting are the public narratives. All mainstream news, including Fox News, continue to push finality—the idea that the election is over and decided, when it is in fact in dispute and when it has not yet been finalized. The Trump team responds by pushing evidence—strangely changed rules, flagrantly broken rules, and endless testimonies. As a result, Biden voters are being conditioned to believe the election is over while Trump voters are being conditioned to believe it should not be over. The only assurance is limbo.

If Trump wins, the Democratic base is preconditioned for nation-wide meltdown while the Republican base is preconditioned for the in-your-face exhilaration worthy of a Rocky movie ending. That leads to the greatest danger: an overly-trusted Republican Party. That was Trump's danger from the onset.

The suspicious part is how well the Democrats in Washington played along to make it all possible. Sooner or later, people will figure it out. Some are already starting to.

Cadence of Conflict: Asia, December 21

Readers still can't get a break from bad news of China. More Chinese companies are added to the notorious "entities list". The WHO sends a team to China, which isn't exactly wonderful press. China is the biggest military threat. The US Navy along with the Coast Guard must reshape its strategy to protect against the Chinese. Trump even blames the Chinese for a recent cyber attack.

As China continues in headlines as the villain, Taiwan is evermore adorable. The Taiwanese plan to become their own military supplier and submarine maker, not as much dependent on the US. They hope to get so many awesome weapons of their own, other nations will want to buy weapons from the Taiwanese, who can defend themselves against the great China, after all. As if that's not enough to irritate Beijing, Washington will start calling Taiwan's not-embassy by "Taiwan" instead of "Taipei Economic and Cultural".

But, how serious is Taiwan about its own defense? While Washington cozies up to Taiwan with somewhat more, semi-respectful names, America's envoy to Taiwan is still called "American Institute in Taiwan". And, as much as Taiwan claims to want technology and good relations with other nations, xenophobic immigration laws are still on the books. Immigrants to Taiwan vs immigrants from Taiwan have a much more difficult path and the ratios are insultingly low. Very few Westerners can contribute to Taiwan's economy, technology, and goal of English as a second official language with these unchanged restrictions in Taiwan's immigration policies. Nearly all changes in Taiwan and in Washington go little beyond symbolic.

Washington is mostly talk. Taiwan is too ambivalent to love actually. And, Beijing is easily insulted. The trends aren't subtle anymore. They used to be five years ago, but they're just not subtle anymore—quite the opposite.

Encore of Revival: America, December 28

Trump signed the $600 stimulus bill, but with a "rescission" order. In other words, he is forcing Congress to discuss and deliberate on spending certain items or else the bill won't become law for another 45 days.

Trump's method is ingenious, though many worms in Washington wrongly project their own motives of immaturity or ego. After all the squawk Trump gave about $2,000 checks, the people expect more money and Congress has an easy way to give more money. Either way, many Democratic voters will thank Trump. If the bill is not revised to give Americans more money, Congress will become very unpopular. Violence only increases; consider Nashville. At a time when Congress may need to choose the president due to a failed electoral college, Congress needs popularity anywhere it can get it.

Yes, Congress may indeed end up choosing the president. Senators and representatives from any of 18 likely states could easily dispute the electoral college. Then the Senate, led by the man running for Vice President, would oversee the discussion. If discussion delays, the electoral college fails and is no longer relevant. Senators and state delegates in the House, both dominant Republicans, would then have to choose Trump and Pence to avoid political suicide. With Trump having played his recent popularity game over the economic stimulus, things seem to trend in that direction.

Thanks to Trump, Congress has the power to increase spending and choose Trump as the next president, and Congress has such a mandate from the people. But, historically, consider the factor of surprise. History is always full of surprises and unexpected victories. By the expectations of conventional wisdom, which usually leads people to be surprised by reality, Biden's victory seems too non-surprising not to not happen.

Cadence of Conflict: Asia, December 28

Anymore, it's not only bad news about China, but continued action in both military and trade. The pressure Washington puts on Beijing keeps finding new ways to keep turning up. Sanctions continue to increase. Military attention rises. And, Japan puts pressure on Biden to decry the "aggressive China", calling Taiwan the next, likely target.

Just the same, Taiwan continues as the poster boy, especially with the pandemic China takes the blame for. Just when the Chinese government thinks they get a break, the opposition simply moved and grew. Western powers have effectively sneaked up on the Chinese, whose policies isolate them from the experience necessary to understand Western thinking. Western news audiences are being conditioned to support military action against China, no matter which party advocates it. As news watchers, we must see this trend as it has snowballed over the last decade. The Western world is moving toward war against China as Russia remains safely out of the spotlight.

###

About the Author

Jesse Steele is an American writer in Asia who wears many hats. He learned piano as a kid, studied Bible in college, and currently does podcasting, web contenting, cloud control, and brand design. He likes golf, water, speed, music, kung fu, art, and stories.

Jesse owns various brands, occasionally teaches writing and piano, and preaches the evangels of Linux, Open-Source, and Jesus.

Poetry is code.™

books@jessesteele.com
books.jessesteele.com